Linux Clue

I0000513

Lawson Hanson

Contents

Chapter 1

Where to start?

Like the warnings we read these days on both commercial and Open Source products — this work comes with no warranty whatsoever, and it should not be construed as fit for any particular purpose.

None of that withstanding — you can assume the author has derived much satisfying experience and personal pleasure from using the tidbits of information he writes about.

I have used Linux for three (3) decades and do not use any of the other widespread commercial personal computer operating systems.

Am I nuts? I don't think so. Different? Yes, no doubt.

What I write here is *"Linux user"* in nature and will need to get filtered by your own value sieve.

Some items could lead nowhere of interest to you or could lead to a dead end street or a blind alley which can prove to be a waste of time.

For that I apologise unreservedly. I mean no harm and I did not intend to waste your time with my ramblings.

Is it a good idea to stop reading before you get too far? Naw!

The information is general purpose.

There's no consideration given to any predefined use — other than to show how I enjoy using Linux — in the hope that you can too.

I hope you find passing fascination here and there. I wish you well.

If you discover anything that has promise — to your way of thinking — please conduct your own rigorous testing and evaluation.

I hope some of what you read can stimulate your own thinking or a deeper consideration of the subject matter.

If you see nothing of any value then please remember — I did fore-warn you of the potential for that outcome.

Linux resounds with my ways of thinking because it embodies a generous and flexible user command environment — powerful enough to get run on supercomputers and yet it can fit with ease on our personal computers.

Using Linux is never a chore — it's a sheer delight.

Chapter 2

Getting Linux

Please skip this chapter if you already have Linux installed —
unless you want to update Linux on an old PC.

If we perform an Internet search for 'Linux distro' we find
there's a host of different distributions.

These have names like 'Debian', 'Fedora', 'Linux Mint',
'Open-SUSE', 'Ubuntu' — and more.

Which one should we choose?

There's a wide range of configurations from which to choose.
There are special Linux systems set up as audio and/or
video workstations and with other special focus in what their
developers call *"studio"* systems.

If this is our first attempt to try Linux — I suggest we could
start here:

```
https://ubuntu.com/download/desktop
```

This web page contains an easy to use set of instructions
about how to download and install the Ubuntu Linux
"Desktop" system.

See the 'How To Install' link *before* you select the 'Download' link.

There's a 'Follow the step-by-step tutorial' link too.

The last time I tried this I downloaded a 5.9 GB file named:

ubuntu-24.04.2-desktop-amd64.iso

Get the latest LTS version number and the correct type for your PC.

This is a most capable Linux distribution code named *"Nimble Numbat"* in which we can find applications for music and graphics and video and the Libre Office suite for word processing and spread sheets and the like.

There's a choice of web browsers and email client programs and hundreds of the short mnemonic commands I love to use in a Terminal window, too.

Ubuntu has been in continuous development for over 20 years. It includes stable LTS — Long Term Support versions that I find helpful as my Linux working platform.

Please Note: At 5.9 GB in size the '.iso' file will NO LONGER fit on a single-layer DVD optical disk.

The information at that web page contains instructions to help us create a boot-able USB stick — they say it needs to be 12 GB or more.

They suggest using a free program called "balenaEtcher" to *"burn"* that ".iso" file onto a USB stick. This program can run on Apple computers and on Windows computers and on Linux computers.

On my existing Linux computer I pointed a web browser to this URL:

https://etcher.balena.io/

where I downloaded a ".zip" file called:

```
balenaEtcher-linux-x64-2.1.2.zip
```

Note: If you do not yet use Linux you will need to download the correct file for your computer and follow the associated instructions for that.

Next I unzipped that downloaded file into a temporary directory and ran the 'balena-etcher' process using these commands:

```
$ cd Downloads
$ mkdir tmpEtcher
$ cd tmpEtcher
$ unzip
../balenaEtcher-linux-x64-2.1.2.zip
$ ./balenaEtcher-linux-x64/balena-etcher
```

Note: The leading '$' symbol is my system prompt — don't type those.

The "balena-etcher" process requested my password to give it permission to run and it started up as expected.

When I plugged in my USB stick the system popped up a File Browser showing the new USB device I had added for my use.

This also became the default device for the "balena-etcher" Flash process.

Next in the 'balena-etcher' process I navigated to the downloaded "ubuntu-24.04.2-desktop-amd64.iso" file in my Downloads directory or folder and selected that.

I then selected the 'Flash' button and a progress indicator displayed the percent complete for the file transfer process used to make the boot-able USB stick for me.

That took six (6) minutes to complete on my PC and then I closed the 'balena-etcher' process.

In the File Browser that had popped up when I plugged in the USB stick I chose to Eject the USB stick to ensure all file data buffers got flushed before its physical removal.

That Ubuntu web page has instructions describing how to boot our computer from the USB stick.

If it does not boot from that straight away we could need to make a change in the BIOS to help our computer boot from a USB device.

Pressing the F12 key (on other systems it could be F2 or F10 or Esc) should display the system boot menu where we can navigate to the boot device selection panel. On a laptop PC — I needed to press a small button to get to that part of the BIOS.

When we get our system to boot from the new boot-able Linux USB stick a menu will soon appear asking us to select our language.

Next we can select from any of the accessibility settings we require or choose to use.

We get prompted to select our keyboard layout.

Another prompt wants to connect to a network to let Ubuntu download updates and any third party drivers our computer could need.

Next we can choose to either "try" Ubuntu or "install" Ubuntu on our computer.

If this is your first trial with Linux then I suggest selecting the "try" Ubuntu mode first. That will load up a live demonstration of Ubuntu for you to explore without making any changes to your PC.

Using the demonstration or "try" Ubuntu mode we will find our display changes to provide the Ubuntu desktop menus and task bar to let us look around at the features of Linux to see if it appeals to us and let us decide if it appears useful and is ready for our use.

I hope you will like what you find.

In Ubuntu Linux we first see a task bar across the top of the screen and a quick start menu of items down the left side.

Moving our mouse pointer down over the icons in the quick start menu at the left side will display the name of each one.

On my installation I found 'Firefox', 'Thunderbird Mail', 'Files', 'Rhythmbox', 'LibreOffice Writer', 'App Center', 'Help' and 'Trash'.

One of those icons is 'Files' and appears like a Filing Cabinet — click on that to open the File Browser. This opens our Home folder.

This should look familiar and will operate in similar ways to what we see in other computer systems.

There's a series of sub-folders with names like 'Desktop', 'Documents', 'Downloads', 'Music', 'Pictures', 'Public', 'snap', 'Templates', and 'Videos'.

Initially these will be empty place holders, except for 'snap' that contains sub-folders for 'firefox' and 'snapd desktop integration'.

Click on the [x] button at the top right side to close the File Browser window.

Another of those quick start icons is 'LibreOffice Writer'. If we click on that we will soon see a powerful Word Processor application window. I expect the menus and toolbars will appear familiar and operate like other products we have seen.

Close the window again by selecting the [x] button at the top right side or by selecting the 'Exit LibreOffice' option in its 'File' menu.

At the bottom left side of the main Ubuntu window is an item called 'Show Apps'. If we select that we will see a collection of the application programs the demo or 'try' version of Ubuntu has loaded.

Try one or two other items — like 'Clocks' or 'Calculator' or 'Calendar' or 'Text Editor'.

Ubuntu Linux is highly polished and provides the user with an extensive array of tools. The installation process has loaded a small sample of those.

At best we have scratched the surface with the soft end of a feather.

If we want to take Linux further we can either — install Linux "alongside" our current system — making it a dual boot system or we can — install Linux "in place of" our current system — caution.

That is okay if we are ready and want to replace the old operating system.

Are there any files on our current system we need to keep?

Ensure you make a backup of those onto removable media before you overwrite your disk with a new Linux installation.

Reversing that process is not covered here. It can be impossible if you did not backup your files. You will need to search for details about how to attempt that.

Please read the Ubuntu notes before you go too far.

If you are certain you want to install Ubuntu then you can

return to the installer menu by selecting the Install Ubuntu shortcut icon on the desktop.

I was using an old PC and needed to re-boot the computer and the select the 'safe graphics' option to let me get through the installation process.

If your computer device has *another* operating system installed on it then you should see an option to let you install Ubuntu alongside that system instead of replacing it.

If you want Ubuntu Linux to be the *single* operating system on your hard drive then select Erase disk and install Ubuntu.

Follow the prompts and select the defaults unless you know why you need to choose an alternative option.

Good luck.

Chapter 3

Linux user

I spend untold hours working away at my Linux computer.

As I write the text for this book — I am using Linux.

Last century in the 1980's I started using the Unix computer operating system when I worked at C.S.I.R.O. and have never looked back.

The scientists and technologists like myself found we were able to get more work done on Unix than we had ever managed to achieve before on other systems.

Linus B. Torvalds was a student at the University of Helsinki, Finland in 1991 when he started developing Linux — over 30 years ago.

Unix and now Linux are multi-user systems and each user gets their own *"home"* directory or folder from which they can assemble their own collections of files in any order that makes sense to them.

In 2025 the Linux system is still the *"operating system of choice"* for most of the world's largest and most capable supercomputer systems with compute clusters supporting thousands — now millions of CPU cores.

The powerful Linux operating system is small enough to run on most PCs with at least 4 GB of RAM and 250 GB of disk — get more memory and SSD storage if you can.

It's easy to add more user accounts to your Linux PC system to give other family members access to Linux if needed.

The files for each user get kept in their own separate area in the computer storage — we'll look at that in due course.

Unlike the popular commercial computer systems where the user interacts most often through the use of a *"mouse"* pointing device to select files and run application programs that each have their own *"icons"* — the Linux system enables *both* that form of interface *and* it supports a flexible text based command interface that people like me find easy to use and more productive.

Why? Instead of needing to locate the file and program icons and grab the mouse to push the mouse pointer around the screen to select and double click those objects to make my intentions known, I can spend my time with my fingers over my keyboard and find it easier to type short *mnemonic* commands and names of the files I want to use into a 'Terminal' window.

That sounds a bit *"Old school"* and in one sense — true. I have been using this style of working on my computer for a long time. I have tried other computer systems and always find myself setting those aside and getting back to my more productive Linux Terminal.

Is that because we can't teach this *"old dog"* any new tricks? I don't think that — I learn something new almost every day — I firmly believe the Terminal interface is more productive.

I *"talk"* to my computer from my keyboard using an interactive shell command language that provides me with enormous computing capability including short-hand methods and programmability features to help me achieve my own array of activity.

What gives Linux its edge? What makes it unique?

3.1   File system and process

The computation model upon which Unix and Linux got designed and built contains two important concepts.

Once we understand these two concepts of a *"file system"* and a *"process"* we know everything we need — to make rapid progress.

I expect you know we store information in *"files"* and we keep those files in collections of *"directories"* or *"folders"* to help us locate the files we need.

It makes sense to keep information organised rather than scattered around all over the place — or worse — keeping everything in one enormous area with no differentiation or delineation.

We do not want to be playing *"Find the needle in a haystack"* every time we need to locate a report or a memo or a data file or a computer script.

On my computer I use a series of directory or folder names with any number of sub-directory or sub-folder levels I need to make information easy for me to find. We will take a closer look at how to do that soon.

In a nut shell it's these capabilities the *"file system"* helps to provide and maintain for us — complete with file access control permissions to help keep information under our own control — at the base level.

We could use data encryption methods for more complex forms of security if this need should get determined.

A "`process`" is an instance of a *running* program that got loaded into the computer's memory to perform its action(s) for us.

Not every *process* in Linux is a '`one-size-fits-all`' or stand alone application — there's more flexibility here.

The Linux user has access to easy to use mechanisms in an interactive and programmable shell process to enable us to connect the output of one process into the input of another process — ad-infinitum if such a process chain makes sense.

These interconnect features of the '`process`' allow us to construct our own custom made process *pipelines* to run tasks with both repeatability and reliability that is difficult to achieve on other computer systems.

We do not need to understand every squeaky detail.

In later sections we will inspect helpful features of both of those Linux system design concepts.

3.2   Mnemonic commands

Working in a Terminal window the executable *programs* or *commands* in Linux often have what look like *unusual* file names. At first they appear almost cryptic.

After 5 or 10 minutes these start to make sense.

Most of the command programs that started their development in the older Unix environment got given short "*mnemonic*" names — chosen to assist our memory recall.

By the way — the term '*mnemonic*' starts with a silent 'm' and gets pronounced with three syllables as '`nem-on-ic`' or '`ne-mon-ic`'.

Short names helped to reduce the amount of typing needed

14

on the clunky old *mechanical* Teletype keyboard consoles they had to use back then.

For example the command "ls" is mnemonic for *"list"* or *"listing"* and will display a list of the names of the file system objects located in our *current "directory"* or *"folder"* — or elsewhere if we so direct it.

How do we know what is that *current directory* or *folder* or file system workspace?

When we first sign in to our Linux system that will be our designated user *"home"* directory.

There's a *command* called "pwd" — mnemonic for *"print working directory"* and it displays that information for us.

Another *command* called "cd" — mnemonic for *"change directory"* enables us to change our current point of focus in the file system to any other directory or folder we choose — if we have permission to do so.

After using the 'cd' command to move around to different locations in the file system we could wonder where we have ended up — run 'pwd' again.

Like these three commands the hundreds of software tools we have at our finger tips in Linux each do one task and do that with precision.

It's a bit like when we first started to learn to read — as a child.

At first every word is a mystery — we can't discern its syllables — we don't know how to say a word — we don't know what it means.

With time and practise we begin to recognise words we have learned and can vocalise and find we can understand and make sense of what we read.

Before long we can read phrases and sentences and

paragraphs and sections and chapters and entire story books.

It's the same with this powerful and descriptive part of Linux.

After a while those *mnemonic* command names start to get easy to remember and can help us achieve more work in less time.

We find we can visualise a series of these short, sharp, unique, mnemonic command names to help us do the tasks we need to get done.

The power of computing with Linux gets provided by the almost endless ways in which we can combine commands like these to make our own more efficient commands — customised to the way we need to work.

In both Unix and in Linux this flexibility continues to astound me.

3.3   Terminal power

These days the 'Terminal' windows support extra *"tabs"* or sub-windows and I can have five or six or more of those open in each of two Terminal windows and be working concurrently on different tasks that help me make progress on the work I plan to achieve.

In Terminal windows like 'gnome-terminal' and one called 'LXTerminal' that I prefer to use its easy to open new tabs with the three key control code {Ctrl}+{Shift}+{T}.

We can switch between the tabs using two key codes like {Alt}+{1}, {Alt}+{2}, {Alt}+{3}, etc. Or we can click on one of the tabs if we have the computer mouse device in hand.

For example, in one of the 'tabs' in a Terminal window I

will use the 'cd' command to change to a *directory* or *folder* where I keep text files for my current book.

3.4 My text editing

I use this sub-window to run my favourite editor program called "vim" — mnemonic for "*vi-Improved*" — a most capable and efficient tool where the edit commands are *mnemonic* and easy to remember.

The original 'vi' editor — mnemonic for "*visual*" got developed in the 1980's by William N. Joy and others at the University of California, Berkeley, USA. The availability of visual display units for computers — "*dumb*" terminal monitors with glass screens — started to increase.

I started using 'vi' on Unix at C.S.I.R.O. and it has served me well for *all* my text edit needs — Fortran and C programming and Perl, R and shell script programming as well as music and book writing.

The 'vi-Improved' version got developed and enhanced by a Dutch software engineer named Bram Moolenaar and others and 'vim' soon found its way into Linux.

If you want a quick overview of *effective* editing and how 'vim' can help you with that please read Bram's seven (7) page paper titled '*Seven habits of effective text editing*':

```
https://www.moolenaar.net/habits_paper.pdf
```

There's a special program called 'vimtutor' to help us learn the basics of 'vim' — it's hands-on and does not take too long to work through. This provides us with the basics of editing with 'vim' in next to no time flat.

Working through the 'vimtutor' takes about 30 minutes — a small investment for a lifetime of superior editing capability.

Note: The 'vim' editor commands are *mnemonic* — easy to remember like 'i' for *insert* text *before* the cursor and 'a' for *append* text *after* the cursor. Even the 'Esc' key we need to press to *escape* from text *insert* mode back to *normal* (or *command*) mode where we can issue more edit and *smart* cursor motion commands — its capability is astonishing.

The last line in the edit window is a *status* line and informs us when we are in the text '-- INSERT --' mode.

We soon get in the habit of pressing the 'Esc' key — it's easy.

If the 'vim' editor is not your *style* there are others you can install and try — like 'cream', 'emacs', 'featherpad', 'kate', 'nedit' and more.

You need to find one that works for you.

3.5   My document method

In another 'tab' in a second 'Terminal' window I will open the same file system directory workspace and this gets used when I want to re-run my document processing system.

I use the brilliant LaTeX system — a set of document preparation macros developed by Dr. Leslie B. Lamport to run on the TeX computer typesetting system — developed by Prof. Donald E. Knuth at Stanford University.

I have used these tools since the time I worked on Unix and these run with perfection on Linux, too.

At present I run this from a small shell script I call "lx" — mnemonic for "*latex*" running through another helper script I called "lxmk" that runs the real "latex" program through the clever "latexmk" Perl script — developed by John Collins:

The result of my two letter command ('lx') is to re-run the 'latex' program on the latest updates I have made to the LaTeX files that comprise my book, then display a PDF file of the *"print"* version of my work.

Next I might run another shell script I call "l2e" — mnemonic for *"latex to epub"*. It's a helper scripts to re-process the book content into an "epub" version of the document and displays that in my favourite epub reader called "okular" — most useful — great for proofreading.

I use 'pandoc' — a general markup converter to convert my initial LaTeX plain text files into 'pandoc' *markup* and from there into the final 'epub3' format I need.

Although that could sound complicated it must in fact be rather straight forward because I figured out how to make these commands work the way I want — and I am no genius.

The best part of this for me is that I do not forever need to *grab* the mouse and *move* the mouse pointer to another application menu to then *select* the menu and run the mouse pointer down a list of options to find and select the functionality I want next.

I do use my mouse device — to shift focus from one window to another or to scroll up and down to read through long texts or to highlight text and paste a copy of that elsewhere.

Those other Terminal window 'tabs' get used as and when required.

A spark of an idea prompts me to add a small text note in my software development area to remind myself about a thought that has occurred to me from my subconscious thinking — or a bug I have uncovered in a shell script.

If I don't act now the fleeting idea will evaporate. I switch to another Terminal 'tab' and add that important note. Then I revert to what I was working on before.

Later in the day Heather — my charming wife gets home from a shopping run with receipts from the supermarkets the chemist and the bakery.

I use my mouse device — to shift focus to another Terminal 'tab' and proceed to enter the main details of those receipts by running my "bills" shell script — it takes a minute or two at most and then I switch 'tab' again to get back to where I was and resume what I was doing — easy.

3.6   Customised commands

What is a *"shell script?"*

Linux includes so-called programmable 'shell' programs and one of those got called "bash" — mnemonic for the *"Bourne-again Shell."*

Stephen R. Bourne played an enormous part in developing his Bourne shell program *"sh"* on Unix to help users get more done with less effort.

Like 'sh' the 'bash' *shell* is both *interactive* and *programmable* and can get instructed to perform conditional tests for the existence of expected file system objects and pass those across to the program processes we need to run to get the results we want to achieve. Brilliant.

When we work in a Terminal window there's an instance of a shell like 'bash' running in that and interpreting the commands we enter.

Instead of typing the *same* commands over and over we can instruct the shell to run a series of shell commands we have saved in a plain text file we call a *"shell script"*.

For any work that involves a repetition of tasks, why not

write a shell script to run those steps in the correct order — every time?

A shell script can start from a simple one or two lines of shell commands through to hundreds of lines of code to help with more complex tasks — work your way up to more complexity.

That's not as difficult a task as it may sound — and it brings with it a great sense of achievement. It's most satisfying.

Before long we realise we have saved hours of time that it takes to forever re-enter command sequences or worse — push a mouse around our desktop to get a one-size-fits-all application to do a task is was never designed to achieve.

Over the course of a year that can amount to an enormous saving.

3.7   More than text

Linux is not restricted to running everything in a Terminal window. We can install and run other application programs to help us do almost anything.

In my spare time I like tinkering with snippets of my own music in programs like the 'lilypond' music notation system or 'lmms' — a DAW (Digital Audio Workstation) that includes a Song Editor, a Beat+Bassline Editor, a Piano Roll, and an FX Mixer with instruments and effects.

We can install dozens of Games like 'Chess' or 'Mahjongg' or 'Sudoku' or 'Tetravex' and others — its even fun to install a module called 'bsdgames' and take a look at the original 'adventure' game!

We can install Graphics utilities like 'Dia' or 'GIMP' or 'Graphviz' or 'InkScape'.

We can install applications like 'Pix' and 'Shotwell' and

others to help us organise our collections of photo images.

Install audio applications like 'Audacity' or 'Clementine' or 'Rhythmbox' or the 'VLC media player'.

Install a selection of modules from the 'R' system for statistical computation and graphics with its 'R Commander' interface and explore the trends or distributions in our data.

Install the full suite of LibreOffice programs 'Base', 'Calc', 'Draw', 'Impress', 'Math' and 'Writer' and work in those — it's our choice.

Note: The LibreOffice applications can read most files like '.docx' and others from similar external systems.

When we combine applications like these *and* the powerful Terminal window with its interactive and programmable shell interface we get what — I believe — is the best computing platform ever.

Chapter 4

Looking at Linux

If we have installed Linux on our PC, then when we reboot the PC it will either start Linux or it could provide an option to choose Linux or our previous system if we chose to install Ubuntu alongside our pre-existing operating system.

During the installation process we got prompted to provide a user name and select an account password for security sake. We need to remember those details to gain access to the new Ubuntu installation — if we chose the option to 'Require my password to login'.

When we type in our correct password then the Ubuntu login process will provide access to our own *"home"* area in the Linux file system.

On first time entry there's not a lot of personal files with a fresh install. There's hundreds of system files like executable programs and software library files and documentation files to read — as the need arises.

After login we could see a pop up dialog window called the 'Software Updater'. It reports 'There is updated software available for this PC'. It has buttons labeled 'Remind Me Later' or 'Update Now'.

If we have two or three minutes to spare it's a good idea to select the 'Update Now' button. On occasion we could need to re-boot our PC to complete the software update.

Updates include security patches or feature improvements and/or bug fixes for the software already installed in our Linux distribution. Ubuntu recommends we let these update processes run when we can.

In Ubuntu Linux we can see a task bar across the top of the screen and a quick start menu of items down the left side.

Hovering the mouse pointer over an icon in the quick start menu at the left side will display its name.

At the bottom left side is an item called 'Show Apps'. If we mouse left side button click on that we will see a selection of the application programs Ubuntu has loaded.

Try other items — like LibreOffice Calc and Writer if you have not seen those before. See what works for you.

4.1   Open a terminal

Find the Terminal icon in the 'Show Apps' area and run that program. This opens up a blank looking window with a prompt waiting for us to enter a command.

Note: The first time I ran a Terminal window on my fresh install of Ubuntu Linux 24.04.2 it gave me an important reminder message:

```
To run a command as administrator
(user "root"), use "sudo <command>".
See "man sudo_root" for details.
```

That 'sudo_root' *man* page explains a bit about how Ubuntu gets configured and is worth reading — one day.

That 'sudo_hint' message gets generated when the 'bash' shell reads the '/etc/profile' file and that in turn reads the '/etc/bash.bashrc' file.

The first time we use the 'sudo' command with success — it makes a new file in our home directory called '.sudo_as_admin_successful' and that prevents us seeing that 'sudo_hint' message after that.

Sounds a bit convoluted — the Linux developers have their reasons for doing that — do not get too concerned.

Getting back to the Terminal window — type in the word 'date' and press the '{Enter}' key.


```
$ date {Enter}
```


Don't type the dollar symbol ('$') it represents the visible prompt in my Terminal window session.

I hope the 'date' command gave a useful response.

Type in 'ncal' and press the '{Enter}' key.

There's also an older 'cal' version that displays the short day names across the top instead of down the left side — each has its uses for me.

I like having quick access to a Terminal window. I open one or two from the moment after I sign in and in general these stay open until I log out and shut down my PC at night.

To get that rapid access I went to the 'Show Apps' items again. Found the Terminal application and used a mouse right side button click to pop up a small menu that includes a 'Pin to Dash' item and selected that.

The next time I signed into my Linux system there was a new item in the quick start list at the left side called 'Terminal'. That quick start list gets called the 'Dash'.

One click of the mouse left side button in the 'Terminal' quick start icon launches an instance of that for me.

If we want two separate Terminal windows we can mouse right side button click in the quick start 'Terminal' icon to pop up a small menu and select the 'New Window' option. Or in an open Terminal window we can try typing the three key control code — {Ctrl}+{Shift}+{N}.

When we open a Terminal window its normal action is to run an interactive instance of the 'bash' shell — displayed in an empty looking window with a certain number of lines of a default width. Initially 24 lines going down and each having 80 characters in width.

Try running this 'seq' command — mnemonic for *"sequence"* of numbers in a Terminal window:

```
$ seq 99 -1 2 {Enter}
```

The number displayed on the top line is the number of lines — assuming our Terminal has less than 99 lines.

If we have a large size screen it's okay to select more lines in the Terminal's start up preference options — I tend to use about 40 lines if I can.

See if there's a menu icon — like the *"hamburger"* icon with an item called 'Preferences' in the frame of our Terminal window. Other Terminal windows could have an 'Edit' menu with the 'Preferences' item.

My preference is to use *no more than* the 80 characters for the line *width* because this can help to keep other pieces of software *"happy"*.

My brain prefers to read shorter lines instead of unravelling what got written in longer lines.

For me that is more productive.

Longer lines can get wrapped at odd places and attempting to read those *wrapped* lines can get awkward.

What can we do with this interactive shell?

We already ran the 'date' and 'ncal' commands there.

This is where I spend most of my time.

The 'man bash' manual pages say it's a *"command language interpreter that executes commands read from the standard input or from a file."*

What is *"standard input"*?

By *default* this input comes from our keyboard — whatever characters we type there — more on this later.

We can type command names like 'ls' and press the '{Enter}' key:

```
$ ls {Enter}
```

The output could look like this:

```
Desktop      Music       snap
Documents    Pictures    Templates
Downloads    Public      Videos
```

When running the Terminal window for the first time it will create three or four extra files in our 'home' area.

These new files get named:

```
.bash_history
.bash_logout
.bashrc
.profile
```

These files get used by the 'bash' shell.

Where are they? They did not show up in the output of the 'ls' command above!

4.2   Hidden files

Notice those four file names start with a dot ('.') character.

We call these *"hidden"* files because when we run an 'ls' command without any *options* or *arguments* the *hidden* files do not get shown — it makes the file listing a bit cleaner or easier to read.

What is an 'option' or an 'argument'?

If we want to see those *hidden* files then we can add a blank space and the *option* "-a" after the 'ls' command name:

```
$ ls -a {Enter}
```

The output could look like this:

```
.bash_history    Downloads    Public
.bash_logout     Music        snap
.bashrc          Pictures     Templates
Desktop          .profile     Videos
Documents
```

Easy enough — the '-a' *option* is mnemonic for *"all"* files.

Another way to list *hidden* file(s) is to provide those file names as one or more *arguments* to the 'ls' command:

```
$ ls .bashrc .profile {Enter}
.bashrc    .profile
```

4.3   Why those files?

The '.bash_history' file keeps a list of the commands we run making it easier to re-run any of those. Try running:

```
$ history {Enter}
```

We can use the Up and Down arrow keys on our keyboard to traverse up and down that list and can press the '{Enter}' key to re-run the command displayed at our system prompt.

This **bash** shell short-hand can be a time saver.

The '.bash_logout' file contains one or more commands that get run when a *login* 'bash' shell terminates in a full screen console.

The '.bashrc' file contains commands that get run when a non-login interactive instance of a 'bash' shell starts to run.

One of those gets run when we enter most Linux commands.

The trailing letters 'rc' is mnemonic for *"run commands"*.

The '.profile' file contains other commands the 'bash' shell uses to set shell *variables* and read instructions from other files to help the 'bash' shell work in a consistent manner.

Later we will find out how to make changes to one or two of those files to help us work in efficient ways for the tasks we want to achieve.

How do I know these details? We find the information in the 'man' pages.

4.4   Man pages

Most commands have what we call a 'man' — mnemonic for *"manual"* — page. A document that describes the operation of the command and has a list of the *options* and types of *arguments* we can use with that command.

We can read those 'man' pages with the 'man' command. For example:

```
$ man ls {Enter}
```

That results in a long document getting displayed inside our Terminal window inside another helper program called a pager or a paginator that will filter the output from the 'man' process and display the long text as one page at a time. This helps us to read the information with ease.

We can press the 'space bar' to move *forward* a page and press the 'b' key to move *back* a page. Pressing the 'q' key will '*quit*' from displaying that man page — taking us back to our next shell prompt.

There's two or three of these 'pager' programs. Back in Unix days there was one called 'pg' and then another called 'more'. My new Ubuntu 24.04.2 installation uses an *improved* one called 'less'.

At first sight the information contained in the Linux 'man' pages can get overwhelming. Don't lose heart.

The 'pager' program that gets used to help us read that information has helpful features to let us navigate those detailed documents with considerable ease.

While reading a long man page document we can press the forward slash '/' key followed by a *keyword* or *phrase* and then the Enter key to *search* for and *move* to that *search term* — if it exists.

If that gets us nowhere — try again using the prefix of the word and refine that as we go — or choose another keyword.

When our *search keyword* finds a match we can press the 'n' key to take us to the *next* instance of the *search term* — if any.

We can press the 'h' key — mnemonic for *help* to let us see a long list of other commands we can use inside that 'man' page display process.

When we have seen enough press the 'q' key to *quit* the *help* list and press another 'q' to *quit* from the document we were reading if we have finished browsing that.

As we could expect there's a *man* page for the 'man' command itself. The 'man' command has a most helpful '-k' *option* — mnemonic for *"keyword"*.

This can help us find a list of commands that mention a specified *keyword* in their command *description* lines.

4.5   Disk space

Using a short *keyword* with the '-k' option of the 'man' command can return a *long* list of man page command description entries — for example a single term like 'space' returns a long list of matching items:

```
$ man -k space {Enter}
    .   .   .
```

We can use a dot ('.') character between words to replace the single space separating two words — to help us narrow down the list of matching items.

Suppose we tried the term 'file.space':

```
$ man -k file.space {Enter}
du (1) - estimate file space usage
fallocate (2) - manipulate file space
```

31

posix_fallocate (3) - allocate file space

A '1' in parentheses in the second column of the output tells us the manual pages for these come from section '1' of the online documentation and as such these are general commands we can run.

Don't try to run items from different manual sections — most of these are descriptions of library files, etc.

If we run the 'man man' command we can find a list of those different sections — like 'System calls' and 'Library calls' — important for software developers.

We can try running 'man -k games' to find a list of other programs we *can* run to amuse ourself — in our spare time — there's often something in section '(6)' we can run on our personal Linux PCs.

Getting back to 'Disk space' . . .

Next we could think to try the search term 'space.usage':

```
$ man -k space.usage {Enter}
df (1) - report file system disk space usage
du (1) - estimate file space usage
```

The words need to appear in that order in the manual page descriptions.

Try running the 'df' command to see what information that provides:

```
$ df {Enter}
```

Too much information? It can make sense.

Command 'df' is mnemonic for *"disk free"* — look at 'Available' and 'Use%' columns. Using over 75% can mean it's time to get more storage.

We can use a '-h' *option* with the 'df' command — to show more *"human readable"* numbers.

The '-h' option will show a 'K', or 'M,' or 'G' after the number of bytes if appropriate:

    $ df -h {Enter}

Read 'man df' for more details.

The 'du' command is mnemonic for *"disk usage"*. I often use the '-h' and '-s' options with this.

The '-s' option is mnemonic for *"summary"* and reports one summarised number instead of one disk use number for each directory or folder below the current location:

    $ du -s -h {Enter}

Or:

    $ du -sh {Enter}

Often we can combine two *options* together like that — not always — the command will complain if it does not allow us to do that.

Running 'du -h' (without the '-s' option) will list one line for each file and directory found below the current directory — that can include lots of files used by applications like word processors and email clients and others — files we never knew the system needed to store for us.

If we inspect the 'man' page for the 'du' command we can navigate to the entry that describes the '-s' option by using a search term like '/ -s' with a blank space *after* the '/' character and *before* the '-s' we want.

Why? Because most **man** page sections that describe their *options* will get set out on lines that start with blank space indentation at the left side before each item like '-h' and '-s'.

4.6 User id

Each user on a Linux system gets their own user and group identifiers — starting from 1000 and is a member of one or more groups starting with their own.

Another two character command called 'id' will display a string of identifiers like 'uid' — *user* identifier, 'gid' — *group* identifier and 'groups' — a list of the system *groups* to which we have administrator access:

```
$ id {Enter}
uid=1000(clu) gid=1000(clu)
groups=1000(clu), 4(adm), 24(cdrom),
27(sudo), 30(dip), 46(plugdev),
100(users), 114(lpadmin)
```

Most of the entries after 'groups=1000(clu)' is a list of system administration groups to which we could need access at certain times.

If there is another user on our Linux system named 'alex' then we can see their user id and groups access by running:

```
$ id alex {Enter}
uid=1011(alex) gid=1011(alex)
groups=1011(alex),100(users)
```

There's another related command called 'groups' that will produce a list of the group names in which the user is a member.

We get a bit less output by running the 'groups' command:

```
$ groups alex {Enter}
alex : alex users
```

This user has no *administrator* access to system groups.
They could need to ask the administrator to run certain
commands for them — if they *need* such access.

They could ask the administrator to install new software they
need for their work and other projects.

Always consider with care what other people ask the
administrator to do with that privileged system administrator
access.

The group numbers and names can — at times differ from
one Linux system to another.

The list of groups gets kept in a readable plain text system
file that gets stored at '/etc/group'.

See: 'man group' for the details.

4.7   Administrator privilege

The first account (the *administrator*) created by the person
who installs Linux gets added to other groups to enable them
to run *administrator* commands using the 'sudo' command.

Not all users on a multi-user Linux server need access to
administrator capability. Such access must get restricted to
one or two who *must* have such access to perform their tasks.

We do not hand out *administrator* access to anyone.

How do we identify trusted individuals who will not
abuse the privilege that comes with such extended group
administrator access.

It takes a while to consider the depth of such privilege.

We need to hunt through the on-line documentation and heed the warnings about the use and potential for abuse of system commands.

In general, administrator commands do not need to get used all the time by the average user — like me — when we are doing ordinary user tasks.

When we *need* to wear our system administrator's hat we should exercise extreme care before we press the '{Enter}' key.

There's no sense in making a mess from which we could need to use more effort to clean up, restore and repair — or worse — re-install.

Learn to make use of the *search* command when reading the `man` pages — press the '/' key and search word — then press the '{Enter}' key.

We could need to know those access identifiers one day — running the '`id`' command displays that information for the user who runs '`id`'.

Note: I was displaying '{Enter}' to remind us that we need to press the {Enter} key to hand over the command we want the interactive **bash** shell to interpret and run for us.

From here on I will assume we know that need when we see a command after my system prompt ('$') at the start of a line.

Chapter 5

Linux file system

The image shows a representation of a small part of the Linux File System — we can think of it as an inverted tree structure.

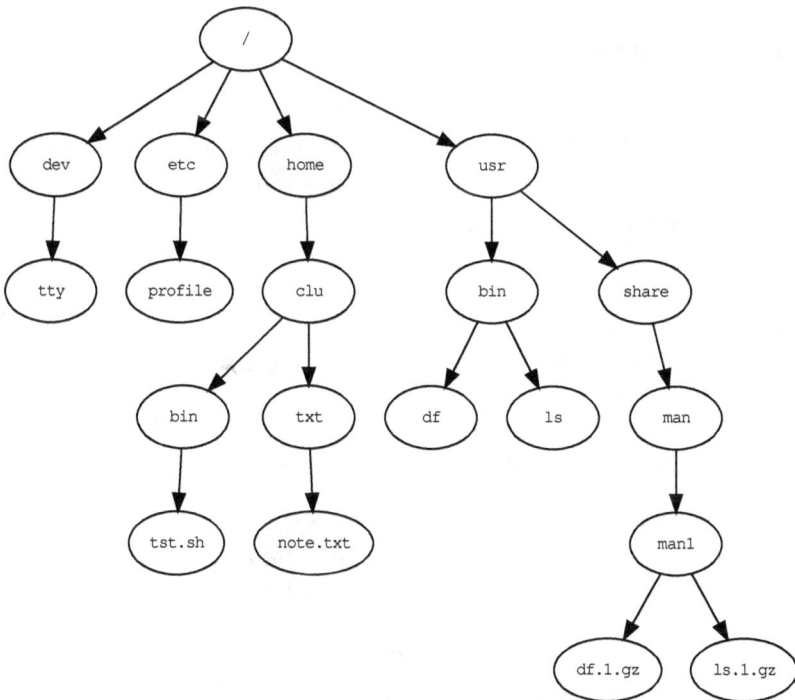

Most user accessible files on Linux can be one of three different types:

- an ordinary file like a memo or a spreadsheet or a music file or a computer program or a shell script or a data file, etc.

- a directory that contains links between file names and directory names we use and their locations within the storage system.

- a special device file for hardware input from a keyboard or a microphone or a mouse or output to a terminal window, etc.

Again, we do not need to understand every squeaky detail.

The top node labeled '/' — with the '**slash**' or '*forward slash*' character, is also known by the names '**root**' directory or '**root**' folder or by some as '*the slash*' directory or folder.

The Linux file system *starts* from that point.

I have shown four (4) sub-directories or sub-folders at the next level down. In reality there's about 15 and more could get added as required when we install new application software onto our computers.

Looking at the node labeled '**home**' we see there's another sub-directory or sub-folder below that called '**clu**' — this is the user name I specified when installing my fresh Ubuntu 24.04.2 system.

You should have one with your user name.

On a multi-user Linux system there's one for each different user and on large systems there could be dozens or hundreds of *user* directories below what we call '*/home*'.

The Linux system manages access permissions according to in-built rules and will prevent us from gaining access to another user's files — unless they make specific changes to the access permission on one or more files and/or containing sub-directories.

More on those details in a later section.

Remember those commands 'cd' and 'pwd' mentioned earlier?

Try running those two commands now:

```
$ cd
$ pwd
/home/clu
```

Running the 'cd' command like that without any *argument* will transport our point of reference in the Linux file system straight to our own user *home* directory — named with a full path like '/home/{user}.

The 'pwd' command — mnemonic for *"print working directory"* will display the name of the location in the Linux file system where the 'cd' command has taken us.

My *home* directory is located at '/home/clu'.

Your *home* directory will reflect your user name.

Notice the 'pwd' output contains a forward slash ('/') character between each layer of sub-directories or sub-folders and we use those to help specify the exact location in the Linux file system.

Most of the system's executable program files like 'df' and 'ls' and 'pwd' get stored in the directory called '/usr/bin'.

The 'bin' part is mnemonic for *"binary"* because most programs in there get compiled into binary (machine code) from the source code in which they got written.

Looking at the inverted tree diagram of the Linux file system, I hope you can find the two I show there.

The 'df' and 'ls' objects are end nodes — containing no other links to file system objects and in most cases these will be *ordinary files* — not sub-directories or sub-folders.

It's possible to have an empty directory or folder. The Ubuntu 24.04.2 installation process made empty place holder directories with names like 'Desktop', 'Documents' and 'Downloads', etc.

Another exception is the object located at '/dev/tty' — this is a special device file.

5.1   Absolute file paths

Any file path that starts with that top most forward slash ('/') character gets called an *absolute* path.

We call '/usr/bin/ls' the *absolute* path to the 'ls' program file.

When we *talk* about the path to an object in the Linux file system it's normal to hear people speaking with phrases like:

"slash you ess are, slash bin, slash ell ess"

This refers to the 'ls' program stored in the precise *absolute* file path location '/usr/bin/ls'.

5.2   Relative file paths

Another way to specify a file system object is to use a *relative* file path that does not start with '/'.

This needs more context.

Describing my current work I might say *"I wrote a small shell script called 'tee ess tee, dot, ess aitch' and copied that to my* '`bin`' *directory."*

Here I did not specify the full (or absolute) path:

```
/home/clu/bin/tst.sh
```

Instead I used a *'relative'* path and said the file '`tst.sh`' is in my personal '`bin`' directory.

I expect the listener will know *"my* '`bin`' *directory"* gets located below my own '`/home/clu`' directory — assuming they know my user name is '`clu`'.

If we use a *relative* path name instead of an *absolute* path name then we make an *assumption* that the reader or hearer knows the point of reference.

We hope they will ask if they are uncertain.

Seasoned Linux users find it clearer to speak out the letter names of the parts that do not make *real* (English) words — like '`usr`' and '`ls`'.

People could also say *'user'* in place of spelling out *'you ess are'* for the '`usr`' part — best to cut them some slack.

We will often know what they mean from the context of their statement.

These details begin to make more sense as we start to use those terms.

For example, we could hear another Linux user say *"I ran the* '*which ell ess*' *command to get the absolute path of the* '*ell ess*' *executable."*

In a Terminal window try running that command:

```
$ which ls
```

What output did that produce?

Is that an absolute path?

5.3 Command arguments

Try running the 'which' command with these six arguments.
Type the line as shown and then press the 'Enter' key:

```
$ which cd df du ls pwd which
```

Notice there's no output for the 'cd' item!

Why? Because the 'cd' command is a shell *built-in* command
and it needs to operate at a lower (*inside* the shell) level.

This is one of those *squeaky details* we do not need to know
all about as a Linux user — until we start to write our own
shell scripts and the like.

Notice those other five commands get found in the
'/usr/bin' directory — as far as the 'which' command
knows.

In the bash shell there's a better command to use instead of
'which' — another shell *built-in* command called 'type':

```
$ type cd df du ls pwd which
cd is a shell builtin
df is /usr/bin/df
du is /usr/bin/du
ls is aliased to 'ls --color=auto'
pwd is a shell builtin
which is hashed (/usr/bin/which)
```

Here we see 'cd' command is a shell builtin, the 'ls'
command is *aliased* to itself with the *verbose* option string

of '--color=auto' and the command 'pwd' is now another shell builtin.

More on '*aliases*' soon.

The shell retains internal information about our current working directory location and has no need to search for 'pwd' and run that to provide information it already knows.

The last line reports 'which' as '*hashed*' because I had already used that command and the bash shell has added it to a special *hash table* of quick lookup commands it already knows where to find without needing to search for those again.

It's nice to know the bash shell takes all the short-cuts it can to help our command requests run as fast as they can.

5.4 /usr/share/man

Looking back at the Linux file system inverted tree diagram — what is that long path of file system objects on the right side?

This is where the on-line documentation or 'man' pages for commands like 'df' and 'ls' get stored.

These are general user commands and as such their *manual* page files get stored in a directory with the absolute path:

> /usr/share/man/man1

Below '/usr/share/man' there's seven more sub-directories 'man2', 'man3', 'man4', ..., 'man8' for each of the organized manual sections.

The file names like 'df.1.gz' and 'ls.1.gz' ending in '.gz' imply these files get compressed with the 'gzip' program to save space.

When we run the 'man ls' command to read the on-line manual page the compressed file gets decompressed and then displayed for us.

It's good to know that Linux is taking care of all those details for us and presenting us with the information we request.

5.5   File information

Apart from its file name and content the Linux system maintains other information about the files it stores for us.

Let's take a closer look at that hidden '.bashrc' file.

There's another option ('-l') for the 'ls' command that can provide more information for us. The option '-l' is mnemonic for a *'long'* listing.

Here is the nine (9) columns of output I get when using that:

```
$ ls -l .bashrc
-rw-rw---- 1 clu clu 3771 May 28 15:50 .bashrc
$
```

Note: The file name and other parts of the output shown above could get wrapped onto the next line because of page width size limitations.

The output from and 'ls -l' command contains these nine (9) space separated *columns* of information:

1. The first ten (10) *characters* ('-rw-rw----') contain a directory or file type bit or flag *and* then nine (9) access permission bits or flags — each one is a single character

   The first dash ('-') character indicates this file system object is an *ordinary* file

44

This first character will be a 'c' for a *character special device* file or a 'd' for a *directory* object or an 'l' for a *symbolic link* to a file — tuck that away for future reference if interested

The next nine (9) *characters* show three (3) sets of three (3) 'rwx' characters — in that order.

These are permission bits or flags for the object owning 'user', the object owning 'group' and then for all '*other*' users on our system

Character 'r' means 'read' access permission
Character 'w' means 'write' access permission
Character 'x' means 'execute' permission
Character '-' means a permission is 'not' granted

Any of those nine characters can get substituted with a dash (-) character instead — to signify the removal of a permission bit from the *user, group* or *others.*

2. The number of links to this file system object

3. The object owning 'user' name identifier

4. The object owning 'group' name identifier

5. The file system object size in bytes and an optional unit specifier (like 3.7K, or M, or G, . . .) if we also add a '-h' option — mnemonic for *human readable* onto the 'ls -l' command

6. The last update month

7. The update day of the month

8. The update time of day in hours and minutes or we will see a 4 digit year number for objects updated more than one year ago

9. The name of the file system object

For this '.bashrc' file we can see the permission bits in those three sets get 'rw–' for the user, 'rw–' for the group and '–––' for others.

Columns 3 and 4 show the owner's *user* and *group* identifier as 'clu' — the user name I chose to use on my new Linux installation.

Those permission bits imply that *user* 'clu' or any other *user* with membership in the 'clu' *group* can both *read* ('r') and *write* ('w') this file.

The *execute* ('x') permission bit is *denied* (set to a dash '–').

For *all* other users *all* permission access bits get *denied* through those last three dash characters ('–––').

In column 5 the '.bashrc' file size gets reported as 3771 bytes.

Linux maintains these nineteen (19) pieces of *metadata* (and more) about every file and directory that it stores in the file system for us.

The permission bits enable the Linux system to maintain control over who has access to the files we generate by comparing the file owner identifier with the user identifier of a user who attempts to access a file.

If the third set of 'rwx' permission bits does *not* provide the *read* or *write* or *execute* access a user needs then more checking gets done.

If a user requesting access does not have the same user identifier or group identifier as the file — or the 'rwx' permission bits do not grant the required access then they will see an error message reading 'Permission denied'.

It's good to know the Linux file system performs these checks according to the permission bits we choose to set on our file system objects.

It takes a user with super user ('**sudo**') access or a *malicious* program with such access to get around those security intentions.

5.6   The chmod command

There's a command called '**chmod**' — mnemonic for *change mode* that lets us change those permission bits (the *access mode*) on files to which we have appropriate *owner* access.

The '**chmod**' command knows about those three sets of permission bits and identifies those as 'u' for the *user*, 'g' for the *group* and 'o' for *others*.

We can follow one of those *set* identifiers (u,g,o) by a '+' symbol to *add* a permission or a '-' symbol to *subtract* a permission.

Then we append one, two or three of the 'r', 'w', or 'x' permission bit letters we want to *add* or *subtract*.

When we get around to making a small shell script that we want to make *executable* we will do that using the '**chmod**' command:

```
$ chmod u+x tst.sh
```

This adds the execute ('x') permission bit for the user ('u') who owns the named file.

If we wanted to add that *execute* ('x') permission bit for both the *user* ('u') and the *group* ('g') owner identifiers we could do that in one step with:

```
$ chmod ug+x tst.sh
```

Chapter 6

Interactive shell

I hope you have managed to try out — or you are otherwise familiar with most of the commands covered thus far.

6.1   Command completion

The interactive bash shell contains short-hand methods to help us run commands with less effort — for example pressing the 'Tab' key to help us complete a command name or file name.

Try typing 'hi' and then press the 'Tab' key.

That could expand to 'history' if there's no other command that starts with the letters 'hi'.

If *not* we can press the 'Tab' key *again* to get a list of commands that start that way.

We can then type extra characters to make a unique prefix string for the command we want and then press the 'Tab' key again.

When that expands to the command name we want then

pressing the Enter key will run that for us.

At times this can be most helpful — not always if there's a list of commands that all start with the same character string.

If we see the command we want to run in the displayed list we can mouse left side button double click to highlight that — then type {Ctrl}+{U} to *undo* the start of the command name we had started to type and then press the mouse centre/wheel button to paste that highlighted command name next to our shell prompt.

That can save a lot of typing when the commands we need to run have longer than usual names.

6.2   Command history

```
$ date
 . . .
$ history
121  . . .
122  . . .
123  . . .
124  date
125  history
$
```

That should run the 'date' command and then produce a 'history' list of the recent commands we have run in the Terminal window.

There's a command number on the left side and the command strings on the right side of those. Expect the command numbers you observe to be different from what I show here.

One convenient way to re-run one of the commands in our 'history' list is to use the Up and Down arrow keys to traverse or scroll the list and then press the Enter key when we have found the command we want to re-run.

The 'bash' shell provides more short-hand methods to re-run commands from our 'history' list by entering an exclamation ('!') character to start a history substitution to make one of the following:

!n
— Refers to command number n

!-n
— Refers to the current command minus the number n

!!
— Refers to the previous command.
— This is a *synonym* for '!-1'

!string
— Refers to the most recent command *preceding* the current position in our history list *starting* with the unique *string*

!$
— Refers to the last word of the previous command

If we need to run *another* command (like 'less') using the *same last* argument as we used on the previous command (like 'ls') we can type:

```
$ ls ~/long/path/to/file.blah
/home/clu/long/path/to/file.blah
$ less !$
```

This would then run:

```
$ less ~/long/path/to/file.blah
```

That can save a bit of typing — or a mouse motion and mouse buttons *copy* and *paste* operation.

Instead of pressing the Up arrow key 20 times we could type '!101' and press the `Enter` key if we see the command we want to re-run has a command number of '101' in our `history` list.

If we have already run that '`which`' command with the six (6) arguments we could try entering:

```
$ !wh
which cd df du ls pwd which
/usr/bin/df
/usr/bin/du
/usr/bin/ls
/usr/bin/pwd
/usr/bin/which
$
```

The first line displayed after we type '`!wh`' and press the Enter key shows a copy of the command that the shell is now running for us and the next five (5) lines shows the output from that re-run '`which`' command.

Run the '`man bash`' command and *search* for the string '`Event`' (inside the `man` page display) by typing the command '/Event' and press the '`Enter`' key — this should get us to a section titled: '`Event Designators`'.

Press the '`q`' key when we have seen enough in '`man bash`'.

I find the item called a '`Quick substitution`' to be useful too — when I mistype a command name or a file name.

To re-run the *previous* command with a change from an *old* string to a *new* string we can type a *caret* or *circumflex* (or *pointy hat*) symbol (^) then the *old string* followed by another *caret* or *circumflex* (or *pointy hat*) symbol (^) and the *new string*:

```
^oldStr^newStr
```

For example:

```
$ lwss file1.txt file2.txt
Command 'lwss' not found, .  .  .
$ ^ws^es
less file1.txt file2.txt
.  .  .
```

My fumble fingers again — fixed with seven (7) key strokes instead of 25 (*including* the {Enter} key).

These `bash` shell history list and command-line short-hand methods get my resounding *tick* of approval.

Every second or two of saving counts in my favour!

6.3   Alias commands

The 'bash' shell provides a method to let us use what it calls '*aliases*'.

Run the 'alias' command to show a list of any that are already defined:

```
$ alias
alias l='ls -CF'
alias la='ls -A'
alias ll='ls -alF'
alias ls='ls --color=auto'
```

These 'alias' definitions came with my new Ubuntu 24.04.2 Linux installation. They have existed in Linux for years.

Read 'man ls' to discover what those options like '-A' and '-C' and '-F' and the *verbose* option '--color=auto' mean.

If we find the colours in 'ls' output difficult to discern we could run the command:

```
$ unalias ls
```

I prefer to read black *printed* text on a white page of paper — and white text in a dark gray (not quite black) Terminal window — I know — I'm *different*!

We can add a '-p' option when we run the 'ls' command to get it to append a '/' indicator character to the end of directory names.

On a more permanent basis we would need to investigate Terminal color schemes and/or comment-out that alias for 'ls' in our '.bashrc' file.

The 'alias' mechanism is straight forward. We use the command name 'alias' followed by an *alias definition* consisting of an *alias name* of our choosing then the equals ('=') symbol and a quoted *command string*.

It's often best to use Right single quotes around the command string — if we need to use double quotes inside the command.

If we define a new alias with the same name as an existing one then the new definition overwrites the old alias — it's best to check.

We can type the alias command followed by the new alias *name* we want to use. If that is not yet defined we will see:

```
$ alias tryMe
```

```
bash:  alias:  tryMe:  not found
```

It's wise to *also* run the 'type' command to check there is no
other *command* or *script* with the same name:

```
$ type tryMe
bash:  type:  tryMe:  not found
```

Otherwise we will see the named *alias* definition:

```
$ alias ll
alias ll='ls -alF'
```

Or using the 'type' command we could see a shell *builtin* or
an *alias* or a *command* or a *script* — if it pre-exists:

```
$ type ll
ll is aliased to 'ls -alF'
```

6.4   Add an alias

Let's try adding an alias called 'a' to run that 'alias'
command. Remember to check first:

```
$ type a
bash:  type:  a:  not found
```

That's good — we can use 'a' for our new *alias*:

```
$ alias a=alias
```

Try out the new 'a' command.

An *alias* is not limited to running *one* command!

We can use the semi-colon (';') *command separator* character
and define an *alias* to run a *series* of commands:

```
$ type c3
bash:  type:  c3:  not found
$ alias c3="clear;echo;ncal -b -3"
$ c3
...
```

I hope you like the result.

The pair of double quote ("...") characters around the
alias command definition is necessary because of the list of
commands and the blank space characters in the last 'ncal'
command.

We want the whole right side to get assigned to the alias
name 'c3'.

We could prefer the output without giving the '-b' option to
'ncal':

```
$ type n3
bash:  type:  n3:  not found
$ alias n3="clear;echo;ncal -3;echo"
$ n3
...
```

I used 'ncal' in both aliases because it highlights the current
day!

Imagine the possibilities — we can define our own *aliases* to
do almost anything.

There's one drawback with using the 'alias' command
in this way from our interactive shell — when we exit the

Terminal window or logout from Linux those new aliases will disappear.

All is not lost. There's one or two ways to make these permanent.

One possibility is to save a list of the aliases we have defined into a plain text file.

The next time we login again we can *restore* those pre-recorded aliases using a 'source' command.

That takes a bit of editing — and remembering to run 'source'.

We can use another more automated technique I will talk about in the next section.

6.5   Bash shell startup

Here I want to make a more detailed inspection of what is happening when we start working in a Terminal window.

On the Ubuntu 24.04.2 Linux system the default Terminal window is part of the GNOME user environment (unless we have changed that).

The executable program is 'gnome-terminal'. When it gets run by us it starts an interactive instance of the 'bash' shell for us to work in.

Other types of Terminal window like the KDE 'Konsole' or the LXDE 'LXTerminal' and the older 'xterm' variations work in a similar vein.

The 'man bash' documentation pages contain information that implies:

"When bash is invoked as an interactive login

*shell, it first reads and executes commands from
the file '/etc/profile', if that file exists. After
this it looks in the user's home directory for the
files '.bash_profile' and '.bash_login' and
'.profile' in that order and reads and executes
commands from the first one that exists and is
readable."*

When we ran the '`ls -a`' command in our '`home` directory:

```
$ cd
$ ls -a
...
$
```

We found we had a file named '`.profile`' in there and from
what we read *above* about the **bash** shell *invocation* (start
up) we expect the commands in that file to get read when
our Terminal window starts — because (for me) that uses an
interactive *login* shell.

On my system I had neither of the other two files:
'`.bash_profile`' or '`.bash_login`' mentioned in the
invocation note.

If we examine the '`.profile`' file we find it contains
instructions to get it to read commands from another file we
have that's named '`.bashrc `' — the *hidden* file we used with
the '`ls -l`' command.

If we examine the '`.bashrc `' file we find it contains
instructions to get it to read commands from yet another file
named '`.bash_aliases`' — if that file exists.

Again — all a bit convoluted for most of us.

In my new Ubuntu 24.04.2 installation the file named
'`.bash_aliases`' did *not* yet exist.

We can use that file ('.bash_aliases') to prove to ourself that the interactive 'bash' shell in our Terminal window *does* get initialised in the way that text in the 'man bash' manual pages describe.

Why is that important?

The '.bash_aliases' file is a great place to start adding our own *alias* command definitions — like 'a' and 'c3' and 'n3'.

Is there already a '.bash_aliases' file in your '$HOME' directory?

Please run:

```
$ cd
$ ls .bash_aliases
ls:  cannot access '.bash_aliases':
No such file or directory
```

If you see the 'No such file or directory' message then that looks okay — the file does not yet exist.

Note: If you have already used the '.bash_aliases' file — please make a *backup* copy of that:

```
$ cd
$ cp -i .bash_aliases .bash_aliases-old
```

If you have the time and/or interest, stick with me and run or try to read through the next five (5) *sets* of commands — as an experiment.

Let's use the 'type' command to check to see if we already have a command named 'h' — it *should* fail:

```
$ type h
bash:  type:  h:  not found
$
```

The error message displayed before the next system prompt ('$') tells us we do not have any command named 'h'.

Next let's make our own command called 'h' to run the 'history' command with that single key 'h' — and the Enter key.

Type the next two commands with care. First the bare 'cd' command ensures we will work in our own 'home' directory. Please check that 'echo' command twice — before pressing the 'Enter' key:

```
$ cd
$ echo "alias h=history" >> .bash_aliases
$
```

There's five (5) space separated parts in this command starting from the word 'echo'.

There's two double quote characters — one at the left side of the 2nd part and one at the right side of the 3rd part.

We need those quote characters because we want both the 2nd and 3rd parts to get passed to the 'echo' command as *one* argument — not two.

There's an equals symbol ('=') between 'h' and 'history' — no spaces in there between either of the 'h' characters and the '=' symbol.

There's two (2) greater-than symbols ('>>') to send and *append* the output of the 'echo' command into a hidden ('.') file named '.bash_aliases' and then we press the Enter key to hand that over to the shell.

Trying to run that new *alias* command named 'h' — it should fail again:

```
$ h
```

```
h:   command not found
$ type h
bash:   type:   h:   not found
$
```

That is what we expect — at this point.

Next open a new 'tab' in the Terminal window — we can
press the three (3) key combination '{Ctrl}+{Shift}+{T}'

Otherwise we could open a *new* Terminal window — mouse
right side button click on the Terminal icon and select 'New
Window'.

In that new Terminal tab or window try running the new
alias command named 'h' we have now added to the file
named '.bash_aliases':

```
$ h
. . .
. . .
. . .
$
```

We should observe the output from the 'bash' shell's
'history' command.

If that did *not* work yet please try to start a new instance of
a *login* 'bash' shell in the current Terminal window or tab by
typing:

```
$ bash --login
$ h
. . .
. . .
. . .
$
```

As a last resort I hope that works.

The new command 'h' is mnemonic for *"history"*.

If that worked then we can — within reason be certain about the string or sequence of shell command files that get read to initialise the 'bash' shell process that runs in our Terminal window(s).

If the 'h' command did not work — we could have made an error entering that strange looking five part 'echo' command.

We can use the 'Up' and 'Down' arrow keys to get back to that line in our history list and then use the 'Left' and 'Right' arrow keys to move the cursor across that command line and double check for any extra or missing characters.

We can use the 'Backspace' and/or 'Delete' keys to remove any extraneous character(s) and we can type one or more plain text character(s) to insert any missing text.

This bash shell command-line editing capability can be most helpful at times.

If you got this far — congratulations.

6.6   Why is this important?

For one thing it means we can add more 'alias' commands to our '.bash_aliases' file and expect them to be available for use in our *future* Linux login sessions.

Does that sound like a lot of work to save from typing the last six (6) characters of the 'history' command name?

This is a simple example to test the shell startup sequence and ensure our '.bash_aliases' file gets used.

I use dozens and dozens of bash shell aliases. They save me time.

They reduce the number of mistakes I make — all I need to do is get the longer right side of the 'alias' command typed in its correct form once and from then on using the alias name — like 'h' is a snap.

It's the 'bash' shell that is *interpreting* the command lines we type — when we press the Enter key. It attempts to '*parse*' (read with care) through the characters we have typed looking for any obvious errors — mistyped command names or other anomalies in any command option(s) and/or argument(s).

If the shell accepts what we enter as a *valid* command then it calls upon the Linux system to run that command for us.

What is a *valid* command?

6.7 Invalid commands

Let's try running an *invalid* command:

```
$ ls -z
ls:  invalid option -- 'z'
Try 'ls --help' for more information
$
```

I expect I intended to run "ls -a" command and missed the 'a' key by one and hit the 'z' key by mistake!

The bash shell parsed my 'ls -z' command line and considered it a possible '*valid*' command and got the Linux system to locate the 'ls' command (in '/usr/bin/ls') and passed the '-z' option to that for me.

It's the 'ls' command that generates and emits the error message that gets displayed before the next system prompt ('$').

6.8   Linux command parts

Linux commands get *composed* from three different parts —
these are:

1. the command *name*,

2. command *options* if required and

3. command *arguments* if required.

We *always* need to specify the command name part — that's
essential.

We do not always need to specify any option(s) or
argument(s).

When we run a bare 'cd' command we use the command
name *without* any options or arguments.

When we run an 'ls -a' command we use the command
name with an option of '-a' to direct 'ls' to display *all*
files — including any hidden files that start with a dot ('.')
character.

Command options *always* start with a dash ('-') character —
or two *double* dash ('--') characters in a more *verbose* form
of option strings.

Often there could be more than one option we need to specify
to get a command to run in the way we want it to.

When we run a command like 'type ls' we use the command
name 'type' with an *argument* of 'ls'. Earlier we looked at
running an instance of 'type' with six arguments.

In general we can think of every Linux command as having a
command syntax like this:

```
$ command [-option(s)] [argument(s)]
```

The square brackets around the options and arguments parts are *not* a part of the command syntax — rather they imply and serve to remind us the enclosed part is *optional*.

In most cases the three parts always occur in that Left to Right order — the command name is *mandatory*.

Options and arguments get used *when* required — to direct the command *how* to operate — or to direct the command on *what* file system *object(s)* or other *parameter(s)* to operate.

Chapter 7

Process ins & outs

In an earlier chapter I mentioned two important design concepts found in both Unix and Linux — the *file system* and the *process.*

In case we didn't notice — we have been making good use of both of those ubiquitous entities.

We know a process is a *running* instance of a program loaded into memory from an executable file found in the file system.

For example the 'bash' shell running inside our Terminal gets found in the file '/usr/bin/bash'. When we interact with bash it runs commands like 'date' or 'ls' or 'ncal' or 'pwd' when we ask it to.

Each of those commands we run becomes another 'process' as it does what we ask those to do what they do for us.

The Linux operating system keeps track of who runs a process and from which of their Terminal windows or other applications a command gets run so it can send the process output back to the correct location.

7.1   Process PIDs

There's a helpful command called 'ps' — mnemonic for
"*processes*" that will display a list of the processes we have
running in our current Terminal — unless we direct it
otherwise. See 'man ps' for more details.

```
$ ps
   PID TTY          TIME CMD
  3108 pts/0    00:00:00 bash
  3120 pts/0    00:00:00 ps
$
```

This output from 'ps' shows the user had two processes
running in the Terminal window or active Terminal tab.
There's an instance of the 'bash' shell and there's the
instance of 'ps' that they ran to get the information.

The first column headed 'PID' contains the process identifier
number. The 'PID' of the 'bash' shell is '3108' and the 'PID'
of the 'ps' process is '3120'.

If we run the 'ps' command twice we will see that the 'PID'
of the 'ps' process will be a *different* number. Notice the
'PID' of the 'bash' shell remains the same.

If we have *another* Terminal window or Terminal tab
available and try typing the 'ps' command in there we'll
notice the PIDs are different again. Each Terminal window
or Terminal tab gets its own *instance* of a bash shell process.

7.2   Foreground .vs. background

Up to now the commands we have been running in our
Terminal window or Terminal tab have all been running in
what we call 'foreground' mode.

The 'bash' shell starts a new *process* for the requested
command and waits while the running command performs
its action(s) and produces its result(s) — after that the bash
shell displays our next shell prompt to indicate it's ready for
more instruction from us.

There's another way to run commands — in the background.
To do that we append an ampersand ('&') symbol after the
command we want to run that way. The difference is that the
bash shell will display our next shell prompt almost straight
away and we can then run another command.

There's a command called 'sleep' that accepts a decimal
number argument for the number of seconds we want that
process to *sleep*.

We can use that to find out a little more about background
processes.

If we run "sleep 10 &" and then within the ten seconds
the command will *sleep* we try running the 'ps' command
in normal foreground mode — once or twice — in the same
Terminal window or Terminal tab we can see what takes
place:

```
$ sleep 10 &
[1] 3955
$ ps
   PID TTY          TIME CMD
  3120 pts/5    00:00:00 bash
  3955 pts/5    00:00:00 sleep
  3957 pts/5    00:00:00 ps
$ ps
   PID TTY          TIME CMD
  3120 pts/5    00:00:00 bash
  3955 pts/5    00:00:00 sleep
  3958 pts/5    00:00:00 ps
[1]+  Done              sleep 10
$
```

We were able to keep running the 'ps' command in the *foreground* mode while the sleep process continued running in the background — until it had counted off ten seconds and then it gets terminated.

When the **bash** shell *sees* the ampersand symbol ('**&**') it reports the *background* job number starting from '[1]' and its process ID '3955' with the output '[1] 3955'.

When the bash shell notices a background process has terminated it reports that with the output '[1]+ Done' and the job's name '**sleep 10**'.

We can have different Terminal windows and other application windows open in our computer login session.

Some of those can be in either *foreground* or *background* mode as we interact with them and then switch our focus to another window.

For example we could have:

- a Terminal window with extra '**tabs**' open

- a web browser session with tabs open in a Google search for a piece of software and a Maps page to show how far we plan to drive tomorrow and our social media Facebook page and . . .

- an email client application like Thunderbird where we are in the middle of composing a reply to an email message . . .

- a document open in '**Libre Office Writer**'

- a spreadsheet open in '**Libre Office Calc**'

- an audio player presenting music we enjoy

- and more . . .

When a process completes its actions and returns any output or error message to us — then the system tidies up and returns the resources it used back into a pool of those available for the next process to consume.

If we find the interactive response starts to get slow and sluggish — we could need to get more RAM for our Linux PC or upgrade from spinning disk to SSD storage to help improve performance.

Otherwise we can remember to close down inactive applications we do not need to have running at all times. Most of these can get restarted in moments when we need them again.

7.3   Imagine a process

Here is one way we can imagine a *'process'*:

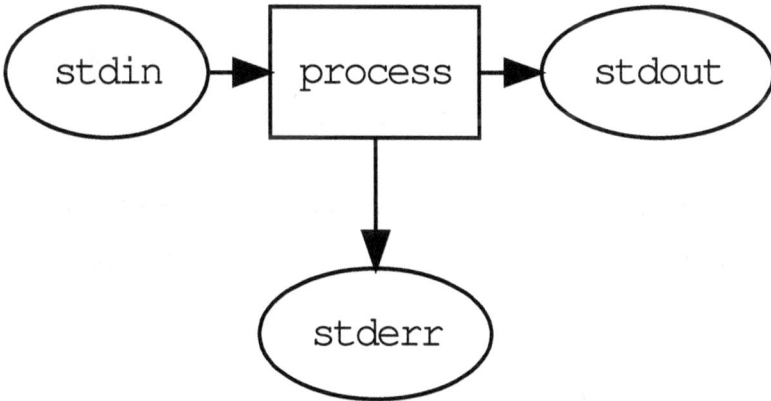

Process Input/Output

Every process starts with three streams of input/output called:

1. 'stdin' — mnemonic for *"Standard Input"*
   — file *descriptor* '0'

2. 'stdout' — mnemonic for *"Standard Output"*
   — file *descriptor* '1'

3. 'stderr' — mnemonic for *"Standard Error"*
   — file *descriptor* '2'

As the *default* — when we or the process make no other arrangements:

- the 'stdin' stream gets connected to our keyboard

- the 'stdout' stream gets connected to our Terminal window

- the 'stderr' stream gets connected to our Terminal window

What other *arrangements* can we make?

7.4   Process i/o handling

The Linux system has more clever design — almost magic.

Each of those input/output streams can get *redirected* — input can get taken from a named file and an output can get sent into a named file.

We use the less-than symbol ('<') to redirect the standard *input* of a process — on file descriptor '0' to get this taken from a named file.

We use the greater-than symbol ('>') to redirect the standard *output* of a process — on file descriptor '1' to get that sent into a named file.

We use *two* characters — the digit '2' *and* the greater-than symbol ('2>') to redirect the standard `error` *output* of a process — on file descriptor '2' to get that output stream sent into a named file.

We follow those redirection symbols by the name of the input file or the output file we want to use.

7.5 Command syntax

I always think of the *syntax* for a command with the addition of *input* and/or *output* redirection(s) as this:

```
$ cmd [-opts] [args] [< input] [> output]
```

Notice the 'input' less-than symbol ('<') points back *towards* or back *into* the command ('cmd') on the left side.

Notice the 'output' greater-than symbols ('>') or ('2>') point *away from* or *out from* that ('cmd') on the left side.

That makes it easy to remember which redirection symbol to use for command process *input* or *output.*

In general I try to specify any command option(s) and argument(s) I *before* any i/o redirection(s).

One exception or variation to that command syntax *guideline* that works for me in my shell scripts is:

```
printf 1>&2  "\nError:  Input file NOT found\n"
```

Here the **bash** shell **builtin** command 'printf' accepts the composite output redirection *duplication* string '1>&2' *before* it's 'Error' *message argument* string.

By default, the output from a 'printf' command goes to the 'stdout' stream — file descriptor '1'.

For my script error messages I want the output to get sent to the 'stderr' stream — file descriptor '2'.

The special output redirection *duplication* string '1>&2' redirects the normal 'stdout' *stream* ('1>') from the 'printf' command and ('&') sends that output to the 'stderr' stream ('2') — where by default, it then shows up on our Terminal window, even when we could have redirected the 'stdout' of the enclosing shell script out to a named file:

```
$ tst2.sh noSuchFile > out.log
Error:  Input file NOT found
```

See 'man.bash' and search for 'REDIRECTION' for more details.

7.6   Redirection overwrites!

Caution: Using the '>' character to redirect output means we will *overwrite* (*obliterate, wipe-out*) the named file we specify as a target — if it pre-exists.

Here's a small example using the 'echo' command and 'cat' utility to display the file content:

```
$ echo "first out" > out.txt
$ cat out.txt
first out
$
```

The result is what we asked the 'echo' command to write and then redirected its output into the specified file.

What happens if we write another line to the same file?

```
$ echo "next out" > out.txt
```

```
$ cat out.txt
next out
$
```

The content of 'out.txt' got *overwritten!*

Please Note: When we *overwrite* a file in Linux there's no going back!

The original file content is **gone** – *for ever* — unless we made a *backup* to a *different* file name or into a *different* directory or onto external storage.

7.7   Redirect append mode

If we want to add (*'append'*) more text to a pre-existing file we need to use a variation of '>' using *two* greater-than symbols ('>>'):

```
$ echo "first out" > out.txt
$ echo "next out" >> out.txt
$ cat out.txt
first out
next out
$
```

The second 'echo' statement uses the double '>>' output redirection symbol to *append* the output at the end of the pre-existing file.

In the previous chapter we saw an example of sending output to a file when we ran that strange looking 'echo' command:

```
$ echo "alias h=history" >> .bash_aliases
```

Those two greater-than symbols ('>>') caused the standard output from the 'echo' command process to get redirected and sent out to that hidden file named '.bash_aliases'.

I used two greater-than symbols ('>>') because I did not want to *overwrite* any pre-existing file named '.bash_aliases' the user could have already started to use.

Using '>>' means we want to *append* the output onto the end of any pre-existing file of the name we specify.

Using a *single* '>' character to redirect output means we will *overwrite* the named file we specify as the target.

Please Note: We need to use caution with the single greater-than character ('>') or ('2>') forms of process output redirection — although this can be most beneficial when that is the action we want.

7.8   Exit status

There's one more vital output from every process — its exit status.

In Linux (and in Unix) an exit status is a small integer value that gets returned to the shell (or other process) that ran the command process.

An exit value of zero ('0') means *success.*

There's one zero ('0') in our number system.

We use other values to signify anything other than complete success.

A non-zero exit value indicates there was a problem.

How do we find the exit status?

The bash shell maintains a special variable named as the

question mark symbol ('?') to hold the value of the exit status of the last command that has completed its operation — exited.

We can use the 'echo' command to display the *value* of the variable '?'.

To get the *value* of a variable we need to prefix a variable name with a dollar ('$') symbol:

```
$ cd
$ echo "$?"
0
```

An exit status of zero ('0') means *success*!

In other words the 'cd' command did what we asked it to do and we can expect our working directory is now our own home directory.

```
$ cd none
bash: cd: none: No such file or directory
$ echo "$?"
1
```

A non-zero exit value indicates there was a run-time issue.

Remember that *invalid* 'ls -z' command?

```
$ ls -z
/bin/ls: invalid option -- 'z'
Try '/bin/ls --help' for more information.
$ echo "$?"
2
```

A process is a running instance of a program/command and can produce output on the 'stdout' and/or 'stderr' streams.

When the process has completed doing what it can do for us it reports its exit status back to the shell to confirm the *success* or *failure* of its actions.

Commands will often detect different run-time errors and can report those using a different process exit status number.

We can test the '$?' value in the shell scripts we write and take one action on *success* or another action or actions when we detect a non-zero value.

7.9   The PATH variable

The 'bash' shell maintains a special variable called 'PATH'. I want to use that to help explore another exciting aspect of process i/o redirection.

Let's use the 'echo' command again to see what's contained in the *value* of the 'PATH' variable if that exists:

```
$ echo "$PATH"
/usr/local/bin:/usr/sbin:\
/usr/bin:/sbin:/bin:/snap/bin:\
/usr/local/games:/usr/games
```

Puzzling at first sight?

I have shown a backslash at the end of lines where I have wrapped those onto the next line for the sake of readability.

We could notice there's a series of colon (':') characters and each one of those separates an *absolute* file system path — like '/usr/local/bin' from the one beside it.

The 'PATH' variable maintains a colon (':') separated *list* of the directories the bash shell will go looking through to find the executable programs and commands we type in and request it to run for us.

Let's use the value of that PATH variable to examine another most helpful part of process inter-connection.

7.10   Pipes and filters

Unix and Linux systems provide the user with another delightful piece of — almost magic.

There's a special character ('|') called the 'vertical bar' or 'pipe' symbol that we can use to help us connect the *output* of one process into the *input* of another process.

Let's use this to help make that long colon separated list of absolute paths in our 'PATH' variable — more readable.

There's a *filter* command called 'tr' — mnemonic for *translate characters*.

We can use this to *translate* those ':' characters into *"newline"* characters — remember those *backslash* n ('\n') characters?

We can put together a command *pipeline* like this:

```
$ echo "$PATH" | tr ":" "\n"
/usr/local/bin
/usr/sbin
/usr/bin
/sbin
/bin
/snap/bin
/usr/local/games
/usr/games
$
```

Please use double quote characters around the '$PATH' argument given to the 'echo' command and around the two arguments given to the 'tr' command.

It's best to ensure there's a blank space between each of the six (6) parts on the command line before we press the 'Enter' key to hand over that *pipeline* to the bash shell.

There is a collection of most helpful *filter* commands available in Linux. We have already been using the 'less' pager or paginator to help us read long manual pages. We will find others before long — and there is nothing to stop us from writing our own *filters*.

What this means is that the ways in which we can compose our own commands has increased a great deal.

When we find a process *pipeline* that is useful we can encapsulate that into a new bash shell *alias* or *script*.

It could be useful to get that list of directories in the PATH variable *sorted* too.

There's a helpful *filter* called 'sort' — that sorts lines of input text.

If the command number in our history list is '1234' for that 'echo' and 'tr' pipeline command we could do this:

```
$ !1234 | sort
```

This adds another pipe ('|') symbol after the 'tr' command and its two arguments to then feed the output from 'tr' straight into 'sort'.

7.11   The tee command

There can be instances when we want to see the output of a process or process pipeline and *also* capture the output into a file for later reference.

The 'tee' command can come to the rescue:

```
$ man tee | tee tee.txt | less
$
```

Running this command will get the output of the 'man tee'
command and *pipe* that into the 'tee' command to capture
a copy of that output into a file named 'tee.txt' and *pipe*
the same content into the 'less' pager so we can *view* that
information, too.

Hope that makes sense.

We can use the 'less' command to read the content of
'tee.txt' for details about 'tee' — it has a '-a' option to
append the content to the specified output file — instead of
overwriting it — if it pre-exists.

We can use the file 'tee.txt' as an example file to practise
our editing skills — if needed.

The file contains a good mix of words and punctuation
characters — in 'vim' we can find out how to move the cursor
to those and *past* those text objects with single key command
variants like 'w' and 'W' or 'e' and 'E' instead of pressing time
wasting auto-repeat arrow keys.

Chapter 8

File content

When we looked at the Linux File System in more detail we considered the metadata the system keeps about every file it stores for us.

Let's take a closer look at that hidden '.bash_aliases' file.

How big is that file?

Using 'ls' with its '-g' and '-o' options to suppress the *owner* and *group* names — to save a little line space:

```
$ ls -g -o .bash_aliases
-rw-rw---- 1 16 May 28 15:50 .bash_aliases
$
```

I like this shortened line version of 'ls -l' and wrote my own *alias* for it:

```
$ alias lgo='ls -go'
```

In column 3 the '.bash_aliases' file size gets reported as 16 bytes.

The 'echo' command we used to write that file seemed to have 15 characters between the double quote ("...") characters!

It looked like this:

```
$ echo "alias h=history" >> .bash_aliases
```

We expect to find the text string 'alias h=history' in that file — or at least on the *last* line if it pre-existed.

8.1   File display

There's a command called 'cat' — mnemonic for '*concatenate and print files*' — a utility to display the content of one or more files.

Let's use 'cat' to make a closer inspection of that file content:

```
$ cat .bash_aliases
alias h=history
$
```

I expect we can count 15 characters — a blank space counts as one.

The 'echo' command stripped off those two double quote (") characters before it *echoed* its input *argument* to its output.

The command called 'wc' — mnemonic for '*word count*' can help here.

When given an input file the 'wc' command will count the number of *lines* and *words* and *characters* it finds in that input.

If we run the 'wc' command on that hidden file we made it could report:

```
$ wc .bash_aliases
 1  2 16 .bash_aliases
$
```

It reports 1 line, 2 blank space separated words and 16 characters.

Why do '1s' and 'wc' report 16 bytes or characters?

What is in that file?

Let's use another command called 'od' — mnemonic for '*octal dump*' to show us in more detail.

The 'od' (octal dump utility) has a '-c' option that requests its output as plain text characters:

```
$ od -c .bash_aliases
0000000   a   l   i   a   s       h   =   h   i   s   t   o   r   y  \n
0000020
$
```

Here it reads input from that hidden '.bash_aliases' file we specify and it displays the output back to our Terminal.

Those zero-filled seven digit numbers on the left side show the character count number of the first character displayed on that line — in octal — counting from zero.

As we can see, there's a two symbol '\n' character at the far right side.

The reason for this observed difference is that Linux uses a line ending character — it's called a *"newline"* character.

This is the ASCII character 'LF' or '{Ctrl}+{J}' or *linefeed* control code — invisible except by its action to move our cursor to the next line.

Unless we tell it *not* to the 'echo' command always terminates its output by adding a *newline* character.

If 'echo' did *not* do that our next system prompt would show up at the end of the 'echo' output line — instead of on a new more visible line.

That two symbol character is the way the 'od' and other utility programs will represent that Linux line ending *"newline"* character.

I hope that makes sense and helps to show that Linux does know what it's doing.

The 'ls -l' command reports its file size information with great accuracy.

The 'wc' command reported what it saw with the same accuracy.

The 'cat' command displayed the file content with the same accuracy — we needed to count one more for the evidential *newline* character — it's hiding in plain sight.

To see what output *without* a newline looks like — try running this command:

```
$ printf "Output without a newline"
Output without a newline$
```

Where did the next shell prompt get displayed?

8.2   More shell setup

In a previous chapter I mentioned that the 'bash' shell reads information from another hidden file named '.profile' in our 'home' directory to help it set shell *'variables'*.

One of those *'variables'* is named 'PATH' — that we have already seen.

In the '.profile' file this 'PATH' *variable* can get *extended* with our *own* '$HOME/bin' directory.

Why is that important?

This 'PATH' variable holds the list of file system directory paths the bash shell and other program and application processes will use as the places to search through to locate the executable commands we need to run.

If we *extend* this with our *own* 'bin' directory then we can add our own 'bash' shell, Python, 'R', and other *scripts* and/or compiled *binary* programs into that location and expect the bash shell to find those for us.

The shell *setup* process can do this for us when it reads lines like these in our '.profile' file:

```
# set PATH to include user's bin if it exists
if [ -d "$HOME/bin" ] ; then
    PATH="$HOME/bin:$PATH"
fi
```

Gak! Gobbledegook!

This has a comment line that starts with the cross hatch ('#') character.

The next three lines contain 'bash' shell *conditional* code to request:

"If there's a *directory* ('-d') named "$HOME/bin" then insert that directory and a (':') at the start of the existing value ('$PATH') to extend and redefine ('=') the existing 'PATH' variable".

The 'fi' statement marks the end of the *conditional* code that started with the 'if' statement.

In the bash shell language there's a 'case' statement that gets terminated with its reverse 'esac' ('case' spelled backwards) statement.

Three looping constructs like 'for-do-done', 'until-do-done' and 'while-do-done' don't get terminated with an 'od' keyword because that got used by the 'octal dump' utility we have seen.

The keyword 'done' terminates the bash shell do-loops.

Congratulations. We can read a bit of bash shell script code!

Too much information? Bear with me a while longer.

What does the 'HOME' variable contain?

8.3   The HOME variable

When we enter a dollar ($) symbol with a shell *variable* name at its immediate right side the bash shell expands that named *variable* to return its *value* — if any.

We can use the 'echo' command to help us see the result. Here is what I did and the result it gave:

```
$ echo "$HOME"
/home/clu
$
```

Remember the first '$' is my system prompt. The second '$' needs to be right next to the 'H' of the word 'HOME' — the variable name.

8.4 More on PATH

Initially that 'PATH' list does *not* contain our
'/home/{user}/bin' directory if we have not yet made that
personal 'bin' directory in our new Linux installation.

By making use of the provision in those lines of code we
dissected above our own '$HOME/bin' directory will get
inserted at the start of the '$PATH' variable.

Please Note: I prefer to insert my own '$HOME/bin'
directory at the *end* of the system '$PATH' because that
means if by accident I write a command with the same name
as an existing system command then I will not clobber that
with my attempt.

I would need to think of a different name for my new
command.

Other people could enjoy writing their own system command
replacements — I'm not that clever.

How do we add a new 'bin' directory?

We could use the 'Files' application and in our 'Home' folder
select the menu operation File --> Create New Folder
and rename the 'Untitled Folder' to name it 'bin' — if we
wanted to.

Bleah!

8.5 mkdir & rmdir

There's a command called 'mkdir' — mnemonic for — you
guessed it — *'make directory'*.

We can use this command to make our own directories like
'bin' and 'dev' and 'pdf' and 'src' and 'txt' — anything we

find useful.

I like to keep my development files separate from my 'bin' and 'src' directories and general PDF files in a 'pdf' directory where I can find them — and it reduces the clutter in my home directory.

To make our own 'bin' directory we can use the commands:

```
$ cd
$ mkdir -v bin
mkdir:  created directory 'bin' $
```

Nothing difficult about that.

First 'cd' as a precaution to make sure we work in our own home directory.

The 'mkdir' command makes the specified new directory within our current working directory — unless we need to specify a more *qualified* path.

The option '-v' is mnemonic for *'verbose'* — and gets mkdir to report what it does.

I always find this much easier than using the 'Files' app.

Now our own 'bin' directory should get picked up by that piece of conditional code we saw in our '.profile' file the next time we log out and then sign in again to our Linux system.

If we want to test that without logging out and back in again we could try running 'bash' with a '-l' or '--login' option in our Terminal window or tab to get a new instance of a *login* shell.

Next try re-running that 'echo $PATH' command again:

```
$ echo "$PATH" | tr ":" "\n"
```

```
/home/clu/bin
/usr/local/bin
/usr/sbin
/usr/bin
/sbin
/bin
/snap/bin
/usr/local/games
/usr/games
$
```

That appears to have found my '/home/clu/bin' directory.

We can type an 'exit' command to close the second bash shell to get back to the first shell.

When we need directories *and* sub-directories we can use a '-p' option with the 'mkdir' command.

The '-p' option is mnemonic for '*parents*' and ensures that both parent directories and their specified sub-directories will get instantiated when we run 'mkdir' with the '-p' *option*.

For example, I like to have separate directories for python scripts and for shell scripts below my 'dev' (*development*) directory.

Here I have added '-p' (*parents*) and '-v' (*verbose*) options to show what this does:

```
$ cd
$ mkdir -p -v dev/{py,sh}
mkdir:  created directory 'dev'
mkdir:  created directory 'dev/py'
mkdir:  created directory 'dev/sh'
```

I have used another short-hand method in the 'bash' shell, using *curly* brackets ('{' and '}') around a comma-separated list of names that the shell will expand — separately into each of those paths: 'dev/py' and 'dev/sh'.

The 'man bash' pages refer to this as 'Brace Expansion' — more on this soon.

The '-p' option makes sure the initial 'dev' directory got made too.

On a new Linux installation I will also run:

```
$ cd
$ mkdir -p -v src/{py,sh}
mkdir:  created directory 'src'
mkdir:  created directory 'src/py'
mkdir:  created directory 'src/sh'
```

If ever we need to *remove* a directory there is a command called 'rmdir' to do that. The directory needs to be *emptied* of any/all file and sub-directory content for 'rmdir' to work — otherwise it complains:

```
$ rmdir old
rmdir:  failed to remove 'old':
        Directory not empty
```

That's a reasonable safeguard.

8.6   Write a shell script

Let's say we write a small 'bash' shell script named 'td.sh' — mnemonic for *'today'* as an experiment.

If I'm writing a new shell script like 'td.sh' — in particular if I did not want to give it the '.sh' suffix I will run the bash shell 'type' command to double check that I'm not trying to make a new file for a command that already exists:

```
$ type td.sh td
bash:  type:  td.sh:  not found
bash:  type:  td:  not found
$
```

Good. I'm hoping to see 'not found' from 'type'!

Let's say we want to use these five lines of 'bash' shell script code:

```
#!/usr/bin/bash
echo
printf "Today is "
date +"%A %F"
echo
```

The first line instructs the Linux system to use the '/usr/bin/bash' shell to interpret the content of our script.

With those first two characters ('#!') we could hear this called the "hash-bang" line.

We will find these at the start of other Linux scripts — for languages like Python and R (statistics) these can look like:

```
#!/usr/bin/env python3
```

and:

```
#!/usr/bin/env Rscript
```

The next line in 'td.sh' contains an 'echo' command without any arguments to display a blank line.

After that a 'printf' (*formatted print*) statement followed by a call to the 'date' command with an unusual looking argument (+"%A %F") and then another 'echo' command.

See 'man date' for information about the format specifiers '%A' and '%F'.

An 'echo' commands always produces a *newline* at the end of its output *unless* we instruct it *not* to do that.

A 'printf' command does *not* produce any *newline* at the end *unless* we *do* instruct it to print one.

I wanted the output of the 'date' command to follow on the *same* line as the short "Today is " prefix text.

Use your favourite editor program to insert those five lines and save them into a file named 'td.sh' — I always use 'vim' as my editor.

If you have not yet gotten comfortable using a Linux editor, there's an interesting *line* editor called 'ed' we could use to construct that small shell script like this — it's not difficult:

```
$ ed
a
#!/usr/bin/bash
echo
printf "Today is "
date +"%A %F"
echo
.
wq td.sh
```

Apart from my shell prompt ('$') type each line as it appears and press the **Enter** key at the end of the line(s).

The 'a' on the line by itself is an 'ed' *append* command.

Next we enter those five shell script lines.

The dot ('.') on the line by itself is the 'ed' command for *end of input* and *revert to command mode*.

The 'wq' line is an 'ed' command to get it to *write* ('w') to

94

the specified file ('td.sh') and then 'quit' ('q') back to the shell.

When we complete the last line it should output the number of characters ('59') it writes to the file 'td.sh' and then display our next shell prompt.

Remember we can use the 'cat' and 'od -c' commands to examine the file content in detail — does it look identical to my five lines?

The documentation for the GNU 'ed' command gets maintained in the 'info' utility and we can read its *info* pages by running:

```
$ info ed
```

Well worth a read one day if we have the time.

The GNU 'ed' editor is a replication of the original Unix line editor of same name.

That 55 year old software logic still works with the same perfection today!

One way to run our new 'td.sh' shell script is this:

```
$ bash td.sh
      .    .    .
```

There's a better way.

8.7 Using chmod

Next we need to ensure we use the 'chmod' command — mnemonic for *'change mode'* to give our shell script 'execute' permission:

95

```
$ chmod u+x td.sh
```

The argument 'u+x' means *add* the 'x' permission bit for the *user* who owns the specified file.

We can test our shell script from where we write it by then typing the command:

```
$ ./td.sh
```

The leading dot ('.') and forward slash ('/') characters instruct the 'bash' shell running in our Terminal to search for the shell script 'td.sh' in our *current* working directory.

> **Note:** A single dot (.) is short-hand for the *current* directory.
>
> Two dots (..) is short-hand for the *parent* directory.
>
> If we 'cd' into a sub-directory and want to return to the *parent* directory we can run 'cd ..' to get back there again — that can be most helpful at times.

When we approve of the script's run time activity we can move or copy it across to our own 'bin' directory.

How do we do that?

8.8   Copy, move, remove

Linux has commands named:

> cp — mnemonic for '*copy*' a file
> mv — mnemonic for '*move*' (or rename)
> rm — mnemonic for '*remove*' (or delete)

The syntax for the 'cp' and 'mv' commands is:

```
$ cp [-opts] source destination
$ mv [-opts] source destination
```

Unless we know for certain we will *not* want to make any more updates or enhancements to our shell script (for the moment, at least) it's best to use a copy process.

Assuming we constructed the 'td.sh' script in our '$HOME' directory we can copy that to our own 'bin' directory with:

```
$ cd
$ cp -p -i td.sh bin
```

The '-p' option given to the 'cp' command instructs it to copy the same *permissions* over to the target file we deposit in our '$HOME/bin' directory.

Without using the '-p' option the target file *could* lose that important 'execute' permission bit we set with the 'chmod' command.

The '-i' option — mnemonic for *'interactive'* — gets 'cp' to warn us if the target file *already* exists. We can choose to *overwrite* the existing file or *stop* the process altogether.

If we chose to construct that 'td.sh' shell script in a new development directory at '$HOME/dev/sh' — and assuming that is where we are working now we can copy that to our own 'bin' directory with:

```
$ cp -p -i td.sh $HOME/bin
```

Or:

```
$ cp -p -i td.sh ~/bin
```

We can use the *tilde* ('~') *meta-character* in the `bash` shell as a short-hand for our '$HOME' directory.

Please note that the shell will not expand a *tilde* if we put quotes around it! Consider these results:

```
$ echo ~
/home/clu
```

and:

```
$ echo "~"
~
```

Using the 'mv' command we find it has no '-p' option — because it moves the location of the file complete with its file permissions to the target file or directory.

If we decided to rename our shell script to get called 'today' we can do this using the 'mv' command after checking with the 'type' command:

```
$ type today
bash: type: today: not found
```

That's free to use. Now to rename the script:

```
$ mv -i td.sh today
```

Or even:

```
$ mv -i td.sh ~/bin/today
```

Next time we sign into our Linux system we should find we can still run our new bash shell script by typing its name — without telling the shell where to find it:

```
$ td.sh
```

Or:

```
$ today
```

if we chose to rename the script.

Try running 'type td.sh'.

Linux does a lot of work for us — behind the scenes like looking through our 'PATH' variable to locate the command names we attempt to run.

When we decide a file is no longer wanted — we should think twice *before* we use the 'rm' command to remove it:

```
$ rm td.sh
```

When a file gets removed — it's gone for ever.

I will often make a 'junk' directory and move fragments of code over to that until I know for certain the code fragments in there got rejected and no longer need to get kept — and I can tidy up with:

```
$ rm -i ~/junk/*
```

to remove the bits with which I've finished.

I tend to write lots of code fragments to help me prove to myself that the code I want to use will operate in the way I hope and expect.

I don't see this as a waste of time and effort — to the contrary it saves me hours of debugging time later — when that process gets more difficult with a growing script size and its increased complexity.

One of my work methods is *"write two"* & *"throw one away"*.

I don't always get to the best solution on my first attempt.

Experimenting with code snippets and making a couple of versions of a script gives me time to assess the code I write and refine what I do and select the best option(s).

Over the course of a day or two the best fragments of code get selected and find their way into the final candidate script I expect to complete and release.

If I'm making changes to a pre-existing script I find it's better to test a small fragment of code to let me prove a new method or way of handling a variable or a process or a file or a logic test — to ensure my proposed code will operate in the way I imagine it should — before I attempt to incorporate that into the pre-existing script.

Suppose I'm working on adding a new feature to my script named 'abc.sh' and I have a copy of that in my current directory.

I have a fragment of code in a file named 'frag.3' that I want to add after line 147 in 'abc.sh'.

I could have determined the line number by running:

```
$ cat -n abc.sh | less
```

Using the 'vim' editor I can do this:

```
$ vim abc.sh
147G
:r frag.3
:wq
$ ./abc.sh
```

This runs 'vim' to open my copy of the script for editing.

Next it moves the cursor straight down to line 147 with the '`G`' — mnemonic for the '*Go to line number*' command.

The third line reads the '`frag.3`' file into the open script placing it below line 147.

Line four runs the *write* ('`w`') and *quit* ('`q`') commands to save the modification to the '`abc.sh`' script and *quit* from the '`vim`' editor.

The last line runs the current directory version of the '`abc.sh`' script to see if that updated code will work.

Did the modified script work?

If it *failed* the bash shell would complain!

Did the update work the way I hoped it would?

That takes a bit of testing to put the '`abc.sh`' script through its paces to check if the new code gets called when it should and works the way we planned.

It's never good to release updates to our scripts and other programs before there has been enough testing done — and most of that needs to get done as soon as possible — rather than waiting until we need to get the updates into production — to meet our expected deadlines.

Linux provides us with a wide assortment of software development tools and utility programs to help us achieve the best we can.

Chapter 9

Work analysis

Examining the command activity from my 'history' list while writing part of this book it seems I have run 37 different *standard* Linux *commands* from those residing in '/usr/bin' while I also ran 30 of my own (*in general*) shell *scripts* and ran 23 of my own 'bash' shell *aliases*.

These commands and scripts and aliases get run throughout my work days and weeks as needed to help me do what I want to get done.

The data also showed that I ran 5 interactive shell code *test* fragments and made 5 different command typing mistakes — my fumble fingers — a sign of increasing age.

How do I know those details? Here is what I did.

I took a copy of my current 'history' list into a file:

```
$ history > hst.txt
```

How many lines of history data is there?

Use the 'wc -l' command to count the number of lines:

```
$ wc -l hst.txt
```

```
937 hst.txt
```

Examine the content of the file to see the structure of each
line:

```
$ less hst.txt
  999   man printf
 1000   sudo synaptic
 1001   tb
 1002   pwd
 1003   owl powerful
  . . .
```

As expected, that looks like a *history* list.

At the start (left side) of each line there's a *history* command
number then the *command name* and any command *options*
and/or *arguments*.

I used a one line AWK script to extract the *second*
argument on each line saving those into another file named
'hst-cmds.txt' — this will contain the list of command
names — one on each line:

```
$ awk '{print $2}' hst.txt > hst-cmds.txt
```

Use the 'wc -l' command to count the number of lines in
these two generated files — there should be the same number
of *lines* in each file:

```
$ wc -l hst.txt hst-cmds.txt
  937 hst.txt
  937 hst-cmds.txt
 1874 total
```

That's what I hoped to see.

Inspected the first 5 lines of file 'hist-cmds.txt':

```
$ head -5 hist-cmds.txt
man
sudo
tb
pwd
owl
```

That is what I expected — a list of command names.

Next I used a small Perl script called 'count.pl' (you can find the code for this in a later chapter) to count the numbers of times each command gets called — thought I'd use the script for a practical task:

```
$ count.pl hst-cmds.txt > hst-ctrs.txt
```

Inspected a small sample of lines from that output file:

```
$ head -20 hst-ctrs.txt | tail -5
bnchk           6
c               13
c3              35
cal             1
cat             34
```

Command names at the left side and counts of the number of times the item occurs in the history list on the right side.

Thought I'd check those first five commands too:

```
$ for c in man sudo tb pwd owl ; do
> grep "^$c" hst-ctrs.txt
```

```
> done
man                    51
sudo                    4
tb                     12
pwd                    20
owl                     8
```

The greater-than (>) symbols at the left side of the second
and third lines get provided by the `bash` shell because it's
prompting us for *more* input — it knows what we have
typed on those line(s) before is still an *incomplete* shell
command. It's waiting for the '`done`' keyword to close off
the '`for-do-done`' loop. That's helpful and clever interactive
feedback.

The '`for-do-done`' loop cycles through those five command
names *one at a time* calling '`grep`' to locate *lines* that *start*
with these command names using a *pattern* that is *anchored*
to the start (left side) of each line by using the *caret* or
circumflex or *pointy-hat* character *first* and the value of the
variable named '`c`' — that is "`^$c`".

As you can see in the output these commands get called over
and over again. I expect I was reading '`man`' pages to ensure
I got the correct information for any references I made in a
part of this book.

What number of **different** commands did '`count.pl`' find?

Count the number of lines in '`hst-ctrs.txt`' file:

```
$ wc -l hst-ctrs.txt
100 hst-ctrs.txt
```

That's a nice round number. Any reason to query that? I
don't think there is. A fluke I expect.

To double check on that I ran this command:

```
$ sort -u hst-cmds.txt | wc -l
100
```

The '-u' option for the 'sort' command requests a *unique* list of the items in the file. Piping that result into 'wc -l' provides the count of those *unique* items — it's 100.

To ease my mind I tried running the same commands in another Terminal window where I had changed with a 'cd' to a directory in my development area.

This gave me 969 items in a new history list and the output of 'count.pl' had 86 lines. Hence my concern gets resolved about that *nice* round number.

Next I made a *copy* of 'hst-ctrs.txt' into file 'hst-ctrs.ed' and used my favourite 'vim' editor to insert a character *code* at the start (left side) of *each* line:

```
$ cp hst-ctrs.txt hst-ctrs.ed
$ vim hst-ctrs.ed
  . . .
```

The command category codes I inserted are these:

```
a for alias
c for command
i for interactive
s for script
x for command error
```

Inspect the same five lines in the edited version:

```
$ head -20 hst-ctrs.ed | tail -5
a bnchk                    6
a c                       13
```

```
a c3                    35
c cal                    1
c cat                   34
```

All I did was add or insert the command category code and a blank space character at the start (left side) of each line.

If I were to *automate* this analysis method I might try to pass the command names to the `bash` shell 'type' command for its *opinion* on the category of each command — I'll save that for a rainy day.

Next I ran this interactive shell command to cycle through those five command category codes using a '`grep -c`' command to *count* the number of lines that start with the same code:

```
$ for ch in a c i s x ; do
> printf "%s --> " "$ch"
> grep -c "^$ch" hst-ctrs.ed
> done > hst-ctrs.nlns
```

The greater-than symbols at the left side of the lines get provided by the bash shell to signify that we have not yet completed a valid command.

The '`for-do-done`' loop cycles through those five command category codes *one at a time* calling '`grep`' to locate *lines* that *start* with these characters using a *pattern* that is *anchored* to the start (left side) of each line by using the *caret* or *circumflex* or *pointy-hat* character *first*.

We'll discover more about those '`grep`' *patterns* in the chapter titled '**Regular expressions**'.

The last line shows how we can redirect the output from that entire '`for-do-done`' loop and capture this into another file — '`hst-ctrs.nlns`' with the suffix '`.nlns`' as a mnemonic for *number of lines*.

The output from that interactive command is:

```
$ cat hst-ctrs.nlns
a --> 23
c --> 37
i -->  5
s --> 30
x -->  5
```

There's 23 *different* aliases, 37 *different* commands and 30 *different* scripts — and 10 sundry items.

These are the numbers in each command *category* I chose to encode with characters (a, c, i, s and x) — and they each have *different* names.

Using another small AWK script to total the sum of those numbers:

```
$ awk '{ttl = ttl + $3 + 0}
> END {print ttl}' hst-ctrs.nlns
100
```

That looks okay.

We could use 'bc' to check the total:

```
$ bc
23 + 37 + 5 + 30 + 5
100
{Ctrl}+{D}
```

Check! These agree.

Pressing the control code '{Ctrl}+{D}' tells the 'bc' command we have finished giving it input and gets it to exit and let the bash shell give us the next shell prompt.

Otherwise we could always do a little mental arithmetic.

The list of 37 standard Linux commands in that `history` sample is:

```
$ awk 'print $2' hst-ctrs.ed,c |
> column -c 50
audacity    epubcheck   ps
bc          factor      pwd
cal         file        rm
cat         grep        shopt
cd          history     stat
chmod       imgsize     sudo
cmp         ispell      tac
convert     less        tkdiff
cp          ls          tree
diff        man         type
echo        mkdir       which
einfo       mv
eog         perldoc
```

Strictly speaking the commands: 'cd', 'echo', 'history', 'pwd', 'shopt' and 'type' are `bash` shell *builtins* — more Linux commands to me.

I run most of those *aliases* and *commands* and shell *scripts* throughout almost every day or week to help me with the work I'm doing.

Can I estimate the frequency with which I run either an *alias* or a standard Linux *command* or one of my *scripts*?

Let's inspect the numbers emitted by 'count.pl' that got collected into the file 'hst-ctrs.ed' and separate those according to the command codes I inserted at the start of each line of data:

```
$ for ch in a c i s x ; do
```

110

```
> grep "^$ch" hst-ctrs.ed > hst-ctrs.ed,$ch
> done
```

Again the 'for' loop cycles through those five command category codes one at a time calling 'grep' to locate *lines* that start with these characters using a *pattern* that is *anchored* to the start (left side) of each line by using the *caret* or *circumflex* or *pointy-hat* character *first*.

The collections of such lines 'grep' finds get redirected into output files named with a trailing comma (,) and the value of the 'for' loop's control variable '$ch' to generate five new file names.

Checking the number of lines in each of these output files:

```
$ wc -l hst-ctrs.ed,?
 23 hst-ctrs.ed,a
 37 hst-ctrs.ed,c
  5 hst-ctrs.ed,i
 30 hst-ctrs.ed,s
  5 hst-ctrs.ed,x
100 total
```

Those numbers agree with what the 'grep -c' command gave when I ran that above on the whole 'hst-ctrs.ed' file.

Using 'cat' to examine one of the smaller files;

```
$ cat hst-ctrs.ed,i
i d=$((365               1
i day=$(date             5
i day=4                  1
i w=$((365               1
i wks=52                 1
```

Column three at the right side contains the command count numbers.

Using another command code character loop to call a two line AWK script to total up the sum of those numbers in column 3:

```
$ for ch in a c i s x ; do
> printf "%s --> " "$ch"
> awk '{ttl = ttl + $3 + 0}
> END {print ttl}' hst-ctrs.ed,$ch
> done > hst-ctrs.all
```

The addition of zero ('0') to the value of the third field ('$3') from each line coerces the value to a *number* instead of the default which is a *string* — an important point to remember when using AWK.

The 'END {...}' clause gets run after all the lines get read and the value in variable 'ttl' includes the summation or total of all those command usage count numbers.

The AWK code gets run on each of those new files named with the trailing comma and one of the five codes.

Again the last line shows how we can redirect the output from an entire 'for-do-done' loop into another file — 'hst-ctrs.all'.

The output is:

```
$ cat hst-ctrs.all
a --> 324
c --> 411
i -->   9
s --> 188
x -->   5
```

Using another small AWK script to total the sum of those numbers:

```
$ awk '{ttl = ttl + $3 + 0}
> END {print ttl}' hst-ctrs.all
937
```

We could use 'bc' to check the sum of those:

```
$bc
324 + 411 + 9 + 188 + 5
937
{Ctrl}+{D}
```

Using 'bc' to check the average percentage of the command
type calls:

```
$ bc
scale=2
324 * 100 / 937 # = 34.58%
411 * 100 / 937 # = 43.86%
9 * 100 / 937   # =  0.96%
188 * 100 / 937 # = 20.06%
5 * 100 / 937   # =  0.53%
{Ctrl}+{D}
```

The 'bc' calculator handles integer and floating-point
arithmetic with ease. The '`scale=2`' command sets the
output to use two (2) decimal point accuracy. It can handle
almost any precision you could need.

There's a total 0.01% rounding down error in the calculations
above — I think I will ignore that.

The approximate ratios in which I run either a standard
Linux *command* or a **bash** shell *alias* or one of my *scripts*
is about 44 to 35 to 20 — that is for every 44 standard Linux
commands I run, I will run 35 **bash** shell *aliases* and another
20 of my own (**perl**, **python**, **R**, **shell** or **tcl**) *scripts* — plus
another 1 sundry command line test or error.

I used twelve (12) intermediate and/or temporary files in this process:

```
$ ls -gort hst*
-rw-r----- 1 20016 Jun 27 09:33 hst.txt
-rw-r----- 1 13457 Jun 27 09:57 hst-clns.txt
-rw-r----- 1  4729 Jun 27 09:58 hst-cmds.txt
-rw-r----- 1  2600 Jun 27 10:13 hst-ctrs.txt
-rw-r----- 1  2800 Jun 27 10:32 hst-ctrs.ed
-rw-r----- 1    48 Jun 27 14:04 hst-ctrs.nlns
-rw-r----- 1   644 Jun 28 09:37 hst-ctrs.ed,a
-rw-r----- 1  1036 Jun 28 09:37 hst-ctrs.ed,c
-rw-r----- 1   140 Jun 28 09:37 hst-ctrs.ed,i
-rw-r----- 1   140 Jun 28 09:37 hst-ctrs.ed,x
-rw-r----- 1   840 Jun 28 09:37 hst-ctrs.ed,s
-rw-r----- 1    46 Jun 28 13:31 hst-ctrs.all
```

The options '-gort' given to the 'ls' command get it to list the file information without showing the file owner and group identifiers (to save line space) and to get the list of files in *reverse time* order with the *newest* files last.

Most of the separate processes I have shown could get encapsulated into a shell script. Some of these could get piped together to make composite commands feeding the output of one stage into the next.

In that way we could do away with most of those files — or at least tidy up afterwards by removing the non essential (generated) files — all except for the input file: 'hst.txt'.

I'll leave that as an exercise for the reader!

When working on a different project the mix of commands I use can change — depending on the tasks involved.

My working environment has over 400 alias definitions. Most of these run one or two commands — on average.

The aliases I write often come in groups to help me with a particular category of work — for example software development for bash shell programming or for python programming or for Lilypond music programming tasks or for my writing tasks.

My script programs range from short ones with four or five lines to others with hundreds of lines of code that can run tens of commands complete with blocks of conditional code to test and determine necessary setup and processing and final results to ensure they do what they got designed to achieve.

If I needed to type out these commands in full every time — instead of using aliases and other bash shell command-line short-hands it would take me a considerable time to do that — hours I expect.

I am not a speed typist. I have a part of a finger missing on one hand and I never did learn to type with any great speed.

I estimate these short-hand mechanisms save me at least forty five to ninety minutes every day — perhaps more. That's from 10800 minutes to 21600 minutes every year — working 5 days a week for 48 weeks each year.

That amounts to a saving of 180 to 360 hours — say 18 to 36 ten (10) hour work days each year — and I have realised those gains for decades.

The 'alias' mechanism is a good choice for running a small number of *fixed* commands.

Our scripts can contain conditional tests like 'if' statements to determine what commands get run on a selection of files or controlling parameters and with the necessary or preferred options to get the results we want and to decide where to send the output(s).

We can write our own **bash** shell *scripts* to run dozens or scores of commands — complete with the ability to loop over groups of commands more than once and with added logic controls to achieve more complex tasks with great certainty.

If I also needed to type out the Linux commands that get encapsulated in my bash shell and other scripts and check the result of every command — that process would turn into an impossibility every day.

By my reckoning I am always ahead by a long stretch.

I'm delighted with what Linux and the 'bash' shell does to help me with my work. I hope you will investigate further.

Chapter 10

Command expansion

The 'man bash' pages contain paragraphs of information describing how the **bash** shell goes about *parsing* the command lines we give it to run for us. We read 'expansion' is performed on the command line after it has been *split* into words.

There are seven (7) kinds of *expansion* performed and the order of these expansions is:

brace expansion;
tilde expansion;
parameter *and* variable expansion;
arithmetic expansion;
command substitution (done Left to Right);
word splitting; and
pathname expansion.

That sounds rather complex!

10.1 Brace expansion

Brace expansion is a mechanism by which arbitrary strings can get generated. For example, 'a{d,c,b}e' expands into 'ade ace abe'.

I used one of these brace expansions in a previous chapter when making my 'dev/{py,sh}' and 'src/{py,sh}' directories.

10.2 Tilde expansion

In Tilde expansion an unquoted tilde character (~) gets replaced with the *value* of the shell variable or parameter named 'HOME'.

10.3 Dollar expansion

A dollar ($) character introduces `parameter` expansion, `command` substitution, or `arithmetic` expansion.

10.4 Parameter expansion

Here are three (3) variants of this:

${parameter}
— The value of `parameter` is substituted.

Example:

```
$ echo "$HOME"
```

`${parameter:-word}`
— Use *default* values. If parameter is unset or
null, the expansion of 'word' gets substituted.
Otherwise, the value of parameter gets
substituted.

Example:

```
$ echo "${myVar:-42}"
```

`${#parameter}`
— The *length* in characters of the *value* of
`parameter` gets substituted.

Example:

```
$ echo "${#myVar}"
```

— There's 15+ other parameter expansion
methods.
— See: 'man bash' and search for 'Parameter
Expansion'

10.5   Command substitution

`$(command)`
— Command substitution allows the **standard
output** of a command to replace the specified
command.

Example:

```
$ day=$(date +%A) ; wd=$(date +%u)
$ echo $day is week day number $wd
```

10.6 Arithmetic expansion

$((expression))
— Arithmetic expansion allows the *evaluation* of
an arithmetic expression and the substitution of
the result.

Example:

```
$ w=$((365 / 7)) ; d=$((365 % 7))
$ echo "A year has $w weeks and $d day"
```

— See: 'man bash' and search for 'Arithmetic
Expansion' and the term 'ARITHMETIC
EVALUATION'

10.7 Process substitution

When available, process substitution gets performed
simultaneously with parameter and variable expansion,
command substitution, and arithmetic expansion.

Process substitution takes the form of '<(plist)'
or '>(plist)'. The process list, 'plist', gets run
asynchronously and its input or output appears as a
temporary filename that gets passed as an argument to the
current command as a result of this expansion method.

Suppose we have two files 'f1' 1nd 'f2' that each contain a
list of words — one on each line. We want to know if the
two lists contain the *same* words — regardless the number
of times each word may appear:

```
$ cmp <(sort -u f1) <(sort -u f2)
```

Remember — no news is good news — otherwise 'cmp' will
make noise and report the first point of departure in the two
unique sorted files.

Note: There's no blank space between the '<(' and/or '>('
character pairs — else the shell would try to treat those as
the *normal* process i/o redirections.

Using this *process substitution* we did not need to use
separate '`sort`' statements with the output redirected ('>')
to named *temporary* files and then run the '`cmp`' command
on those and then finish with the usual *removal* of temporary
files later.

A convenience that saves us from thinking up temporary file
names and then remembering to tidy up after their use.

See '`man bash`' for more details.

10.8   Word splitting

The shell scans the results of parameter expansion, command
substitution, and arithmetic expansion that did *not* occur
within double quotes for word splitting.

This uses the value of an environment variable '`IFS`' (*input
field separator*) which has a *default* value of {`space`} and
{`tab`} and {`newline`} — all three of these.

To see what is in IFS run this command:

```
$ echo "$IFS" | od -c
```

10.9   Pathname expansion

After word splitting the bash shell scans each word for these
three meta-characters — the `asterisk` '`*`', the `question`
`mark` '`?`', and the `Left square bracket` '`[`'.

If one of these characters appears, and is *not* quoted, then the word gets regarded as a *pattern*, and gets replaced with an alphabetically sorted list of filenames matching the pattern.

The Linux bash shell enables us to use these three specific meta-characters to help us refer to file name arguments that can represent a file system object name or name(s) without the need to spell them out explicitly.

Pathname expansions can provide great help to us — provided we learn how to construct the *"pattern"* strings with care.

What do these wild-card or meta-characters mean?

10.10 Shell meta-characters

The '*' — matches any string of *zero* or *more* characters in a file name.

The '?' — matches any *single* character in a file name.

The use of '[...]' — matches any *one* of a set of enclosed characters.

For example using '[abc]' — expands to *one* of the characters — an 'a' or a 'b' or a 'c' — not all three at once.

Inside those square brackets a pair of characters separated by a hyphen dash '-' denotes a *range* of characters.

For example using '[m-q]' — expands to one of the characters 'm' or 'n' or 'o' or 'p' or 'q'.

If the *first* character following the '[' is either an exclamation symbol (!) or the caret or circumflex (*pointy-hat*) symbol (^) then any character **not** enclosed in the set gets matched.

A literal hyphen or dash (-) can get matched by including it as either the *first* or the *last* character in a set.

A literal ']' can get matched by including it as the *first* character in a set.

See 'man bash' for more details.

What does this imply?

For a start, there's lots of experimentation to do to help us get comfortable with what these file pathname expansions can do.

Using these shell wild-cards means we can run commands like this:

```
$ cd
$ ls .bash*
.bash_aliases .bash_logout
.bash_history .bashrc
$
```

That lists any file that starts with the string '.bash' followed by zero or more of *any* other character — and it has matched all four of *those* hidden '.bash*' files in our HOME directory.

We could get more selective and write:

```
$ ls .b*[cs]
.bash_aliases .bashrc
$
```

That lists any file that starts with the string '.b' followed by zero or more of *any* other character — and also ends with *either* a 'c' *or* an 's'.

These restrict the 'ls' command to showing us a selection of two (2) of the hidden files we observed when we ran an 'ls -a' command before.

If curious we could list the two (2) character executable command files stored in the '/usr/bin' directory:

```
$ cd /usr/bin
$ ls ??
bc  du  hd  ls  ps  sh  wc
cp  ed  id  mv  ri  su  xz
dc  ex  ln  nl  rm  tr
df  gs  lp  od  sg  vi
$
```

On your system there could be more or less files there.

As and when we install extra pieces of software the number of files in this directory will grow.

We could add another '?' symbol to display three (3) character command names — there are more of those.

We could add a fourth '?' symbol to display four (4) character command names — there are even more of these.

While in the '/usr/bin' directory we can try matching any *one* of a set of enclosed characters:

```
$ ls [d-p]?
dc du ex hd ln ls nl ps
df ed gs id lp mv od
$ cd
$
```

The list gets reduced to file names that start with one of the characters 'd', 'e', 'f', 'g', 'h', 'i', 'j', 'k', 'l', 'm', 'n', 'o' *or* 'p' — if there's any.

Remember a 'cd' with no argument takes us back home.

We do not want to stay in the '/usr/bin' directory. We don't have permission to write any new files there.

Warning: Please exercise great care when using the 'rm' (*remove*) command with wild-card meta-characters. We need to ensure we have not matched more files than we think a wild-card pattern covers.

It's a good idea to check the wild-card pattern using an 'ls' command or an 'echo' command first.

You can also pass the '-i' (*interactive*) option to the 'rm' command to get it to prompt you *before* it removes each file you have specified.

It's worth the extra moment or two of trouble to give us certainty — at least until we know how wild-cards operate.

If you find the list of matched files seems much longer than you imagined — you can always type the control code '{Ctrl}+{C}' to exit the 'rm' process (and most other commands) to let you reconsider your actions.

I think it's better to be explicit and pass the full name of a file I want to remove across to the 'rm' command:

```
$ rm -i my-old-file.txt
```

That way I get less surprises and my data files stay safe from my own accidental typing errors!

Chapter 11

File naming

I have noticed there are people who like to name their files with a whole phrase or two — almost a short story.

I grew up during a time when every character was a premium. When I started using Unix (last *century*) a file name was limited to a length of 14 characters — and that seemed plenty!

This limitation made for a different way of naming files and programs and every object in the file system.

I still prefer shorter file names rather than long-winded ones. They take less effort to write and they can get named with almost as much precision as any longer more verbose file names — as long as we document what we do.

Why do I mention this?

Although the newer utilities and application programs in Linux will often permit the use of blank space characters and an assortment of any other characters in file names — these come at a cost.

In the previous chapter we examined what we called *wild-card* characters (or '`meta-characters`') — characters that have a *change* of meaning when used on the interactive bash shell command line.

Those *meta-characters* present us with powerful mechanisms to help us specify one or more files without the need to spell out the file names in full every time — to me that is a wonderful time saver.

If we attempt to use those meta-characters in the names of our files then trying to specify those names on the command-line can get more difficult.

We need to make use of another meta-character (the backslash character) to hide the command-line meaning of that character and other meta-characters we sprinkle though our file names!

I find that to be a waste of time and effort — when with a moment or two of thought I could come up with a shorter and easier to type file name which means almost the same.

Does it matter? It matters to me — but then we know I am different in my own ways.

If I work on a project that *'requires'* long-winded file names I would rather use my own short file names on *internal* processing and convert my short file names to the long file names the project *requires* — as I ship those out the door.

A line or two of shell script code will often do the trick.

What others choose to do is their business.

A blank space character is one of the characters we must either *elide* through the use of a backslash prefix or must remember to enclose a file name with any embedded blank space in quote characters like:

```
$ cat 'another blank space file name'
```

Otherwise we could drop the two matching right single quote

characters and insert four backslash characters — one at the left side of each blank space character!

A better method — to my way of thinking is to use the 'tr' command to help *translate* the blank space characters into the hyphen or dash ('-') character when I want a long and more descriptive file name:

```
$ fnam=$(echo long file name.txt | tr " " "-")
$ echo "$fnam"
long-file-name.txt
```

Then I can use the shell variable 'fnam' in commands to help me with tasks such as editing or copying and using the file:

```
$ vim $fnam
  .   .   .
$ cp $fnam ~/txt
```

What this means to me is that we can save ourself a lot of angst if we refrain from using certain characters in our file names.

The three types of quote characters (left, right and double) all have special meaning to the shell.

A semi-colon character (';') is a command separator. If we used that in a file name it would need special handling.

We have seen other meta-characters that have special meaning to the shell — i/o redirection characters ('<' and '>') and shell comment characters ('#') and parentheses and curly braces and square brackets and the dollar symbol ('$') and the like — each have more meaning in the bash shell.

If we attempt to use those in our file names we will cause ourselves more pain than good.

For my file names I choose to use the ASCII decimal digits '0' through '9', the characters 'A' through 'Z' and lower-case 'a' through 'z' plus the symbols hyphen or dash ('-') and the underscore ('_') then a dot ('.') to separate the file name from the file type — like '.py' or '.sh' or '.txt', etc.

On occasion I will add the use of a plus symbol ('+') or a comma symbol (',') for certain files.

I do not find using those 67 characters too limiting. I do know they have saved me from a lot of file name handling heart ache.

Using the 'bc' (*binary calculator*) tool — here I calculate I could generate this number of unique 15 character file names:

```
$ bc
67^15
2461059085914092013369600043
{Ctrl}+{D}
```

Will this be enough?

Not every one of those will be *useful* — I hope you get my drift.

If I were to limit the characters I use to 5 instead of 67 — I could generate '30517578125' unique 15 character file names!

If I were to use three (3) character in any character position of my 15 character file names I could still generate '14348907' unique file names.

I could use each character position to represent a project code or a data code or a process code or processing stage or a result code — and I am not limited to 15 characters!

It's up to the user. It's best to document what we do.

I can use the dash ('-') and underscore ('_') characters in place of using blank space characters. The end result is almost as readable with minimal practise.

I am not averse to using 'camelCase' in file names, too:

```
$ sort bigData.txt > bigData.tst,s
```

That added ",s" suffix reminds me the file content is now sorted.

If I am honest with myself I prefer 'camelCase' or hyphenated words over 'snake_case' for most of my file names — but that is my choice.

People are different — we have every right to be. Following these simple guidelines for naming my files works for me.

11.1   File links

When talking about the meta-data file information the system keeps for our files I mentioned that the first character on each line of output from an 'ls -l' command could be a dash ('-') for an *ordinary* file, or one of the characters 'd' for a *directory* or a 'c' for a *character special* file or an 'l' for a *symbolic link*.

There's two types of links — *hard* links and *symbolic* links

What's the difference? What is a *symbolic* link?

A command called 'ln' — mnemonic for *link* makes a *link* to an existing file.

Why would we want a *link* to a file?

One reason is to let us gain access to a file by a *different* name — or from within a different directory.

The syntax for an 'ln' command is either:

```
$ ln [-s] sourceFile destFile
```

131

Or:

```
$ ln [-s] sourceFile destDir
```

We use the '-s' option to make a *symbolic* link to the source file — instead of a so-called *hard* link.

Those '*sourceFile*' and '*destFile*' and '*destDir*' parts could need to get written as *absolute* paths to the object(s) — for brevity I'll use *relative* paths here.

Let's make a file to play with:

```
$ man ln > ln.txt
$ ls -go ln.txt
-rw-r----- 1 3891 Jul 18 19:47 ln.txt
```

Let's make a hard link to that file:

```
$ ln ln.txt hard-ln.txt
$ ls -go *ln.txt
rw-r----- 2 3891 Jul 18 19:47 hard-ln.txt
rw-r----- 2 3891 Jul 18 19:47 ln.txt
```

Notice the second item on the 'ls -lgo' output is now a '2' for each file — that's the number of links to the file.

They point to one and the same file system object.

How do we know that?

Let's use the '-i' *option* with the 'ls' command to display the "*inode*" numbers for these file system objects:

```
$ ls -igo *ln.txt
32098 -rw-r----- 2 3891 Jul 18 19:47 hard-ln.txt
32098 -rw-r----- 2 3891 Jul 18 19:47 ln.txt
```

Identical *inode* numbers! These file system objects have different name entries — yet point to the same *inode* data structure in the file system — where the file system stores its meta-data information about how it can provide access for the file to which it points.

What happens if we use the '-s' option and make a *symbolic* link to 'ln.txt':

```
$ ln -s ln.txt slnk-ln.txt
$ ls -igo *ln.txt
32098 -rw-r----- 2 3891 Jul 18 19:47 hard-ln.txt
32098 -rw-r----- 2 3891 Jul 18 19:47 ln.txt
32936 lrwxrwxrwx 1    6 Jul 18 20:07 slnk-ln.txt -> ln.txt
```

The symbolic link has a different *inode* number. The entry starts with the character '1' (*ell*) instead of a dash ('-') and the file name detail points ('->') to or is *linked* to the original file 'ln.txt' — it has a name that's 6 bytes in length as reflected by the number '6' in column 4.

What happens if we append extra text — such as the 'date' string onto the end of the original file 'ln.txt':

```
$ date >> ln.txt
$ ls -igo *ln.txt
32098 -rw-r----- 2 3921 Jul 18 20:44 hard-ln.txt
32098 -rw-r----- 2 3921 Jul 18 20:44 ln.txt
32936 lrwxrwxrwx 1    6 Jul 18 20:07 slnk-ln.txt -> ln.txt
```

Notice the update in file *size* and *time* change information for *both* the *original* file and the *hard* link. The *symbolic* link has not changed.

Does the *symbolic* link know we appended the date string onto the file to which it points:

```
$ tail -1 slnk-ln.txt
Fri 18 Jul 2025 20:44:32 AEST
```

Yes it does — we can be certain of that.

Symbolic links use another inode in the storage space.

Links provide us with a method of referring to a file by another name and/or from an entry in another directory if we want.

We can make useful links to files as needed.

A hard link makes a new named entry in a directory in the file system that points directly to the 'inode' of a pre-existing file object in the file system tree.

A symbolic link makes a new named entry in a directory in the file system that points to a '*file name*' or '*file path*' of a pre-existing file object in the file system tree — at first the difference appears subtle.

What happens if we rename or move these links or the original file to which they point?

Renaming the hard and soft links:

```
$ mv hard-ln.txt mhard-ln.txt
$ mv slnk-ln.txt mslnk-ln.txt
$ ls -igo *ln.txt
32098 -rw-r----- 2 3921 Jul 18 20:44 ln.txt
32098 -rw-r----- 2 3921 Jul 18 20:44 mhard-ln.txt
32936 lrwxrwxrwx 1    6 Jul 18 20:07 mslnk-ln.txt -> ln.txt
```

Using 'wc -c' to check the resolved object sizes:

```
$ wc -c *ln.txt
  3921 ln.txt
  3921 mhard-ln.txt
  3921 mslnk-ln.txt
 11763 total
```

They all got read and look the correct size.

What if we rename the original file:

```
$ mv ln.txt mln.txt
$ ls -igo *ln.txt
32098 -rw-r----- 2 3921 Jul 18 20:44 mhard-ln.txt
32098 -rw-r----- 2 3921 Jul 18 20:44 mln.txt
32936 lrwxrwxrwx 1    6 Jul 18 20:07 mslnk-ln.txt -> ln.txt
```

Using 'wc -c' to check the resolved object sizes:

```
$ wc -c *ln.txt
 3921 mhard-ln.txt
 3921 mln.txt
wc: mslnk-ln.txt: No such file or
directory
7842 total
```

Ouch! The symbolic link gets *broken* when we rename the file
to which it *was* linked.

To fix the symbolic link we can either rerun 'ln' to make a
new symbolic link pointing to the renamed file — or we could
move the renamed file back to its original name:

```
$ mv mln.txt ln.txt
$ wc -c *ln.txt
 3921 ln.txt
 3921 mhard-ln.txt
 3921 mslnk-ln.txt
11763 total
```

A symbolic link is an entry in a directory that points to a file
name that existed with that name when the symbolic link got
made — that's all.

If that file name exists the symbolic link is useful. If that file
name gets renamed or moved the symbolic link gets broken!

A hard link is an entry in a directory that points to the *same*
inode as another pre-existing file. Even if we rename or move

or remove the original file the hard link is still pointing to the *same* inode.

When the *last* link to a file's inode gets removed then it no longer exists.

Why would we want to use a symbolic link?

Hard link objects must exist in the same file storage device.

Soft (*symbolic*) links can cross file storage device boundaries — they could point to object names that exist on an external storage device — when those get connected to our computer for use.

Why would we want to use a hard link?

As we can observe above — a hard link to an existing file points to the same inode. Although it appears to show the same amount of file space size this is the file size of the original file.

File links can make a lot of sense when we need to deal with data files that require megabytes or gigabytes of storage size.

Instead of having two separate copies of that we can make a hard link to the real data file. The impact on the file system is one more entry in the file system tree that points to a pre-existing inode.

The amount of space taken up by that depends on the block size used by our file system. That could be 2k, 4k or 8k bytes, etc., rather than more megabytes or gigabytes to store an entire copy of a file.

I hope that made some sense.

Chapter 12

Regular expressions

There's another flexible filter command called 'grep' — mnemonic for *global regular expression print* — that's a bit wordy.

'grep' searches for '*patterns*' called '*regular expressions*' in files.

What is a *regular expression*?

Regular expressions are flexible character *patterns* that can *match* one or more strings of text.

Ken Thompson, one of the two principal authors and designers of Unix, is accredited with adding *regular expression* pattern matching search capability into the editor 'ed' — that we could have used to write our small 'td.sh' shell script — back a chapter or two.

A command we can use in the 'ed' and 'ex' and 'vim' editors is 'g/re/p' where the '*re*' part is one of these *regular expressions*.

The 'g' — mnemonic for *global* means across the *entire width* of each line.

The 'p' — mnemonic for *print* means display those lines

that contain any match to the '**re**' — *regular expression* we supply.

This is where the '**grep**' filter got its name.

A *regular expression* can be as simple as one or two characters or a word — or as complex as a conglomeration of pattern matching characters and repetition counts — as we will soon see below.

12.1   A simple grep

If we wanted to extract the '**games**' directories from our **PATH** variable we can use the '**grep**' *filter* to extract those by adding another section to our **bash** history command pipeline:

```
$ !1234 | sort | grep games
/usr/games
/usr/local/games
```

This adds another pipe ('**|**') symbol after the '**sort**' command and feeds the output from '**sort**' straight into the standard input of '**grep**' asking it to match lines containing the simple pattern '**games**' — success.

You may recall the *hypothetical* history command number '**1234**' started with:

```
$ echo "$PATH" | tr ":" "\n"
```

If the original command output is extensive it could be more efficient to add the '**grep**' command first and then pass the reduced output to the '**sort**' command:

```
$ !1234 | grep games | sort
/usr/games
/usr/local/games
```

For such a small sample it makes no noticeable difference.

Can you see the power and flexibility built into Unix and now Linux commands with the ability to pipe commands together in the **bash** shell to construct command pipelines?

It's almost like playing with a child's building blocks.

Imagine the fun I have been having every day for decades!

We could redirect that pipeline output into a *new* file or *append* it to the end of an *existing* file and read that into a report or a chapter of a book we need to finish writing.

Note: There's one or two subtle differences between 'bash' shell command line wild-card *patterns* and the class of patterns called *regular expressions* used by the 'grep' command.

Regular expressions are more flexible by a long stretch.

There's a lot of similarity in the ideas between the two.

One exception is the question mark ('?') character — in 'grep' patterns we use a dot ('.') character *instead* — to mean '*any single character*'.

Why? Because in RE (*regular expression*) syntax the question mark ('?') character got used to represent either *zero or one* of the previous character or entire RE enclosed in parentheses.

Another exception is the asterisk ('*') character.

To represent *zero or more* '*repetitions*' of *any* character in 'grep' patterns we need to use a two character RE that has a dot *paired with* an asterisk ('.*') — with practise we soon get used to these and other differences.

Like me you could make a blunder or two — re-read what you have tried and realise there's a simple mistake that's easy to correct on the editable **bash** shell command line.

When you get the result you want you can highlight that command line and paste it into a plain text snippets file for inclusion into any shell script you could write at a later date — no need to keep re-inventing the wheel.

12.2　RE syntax

The **man** page for the 'grep' command contains detailed descriptions about how its regular expressions can get constructed by us to match and find almost any string of characters we can imagine.

Search for 'REGULAR EXPRESSIONS' in the man page.

The second sentence in that section reads:

> *'Regular expressions are constructed like arithmetic expressions, by using various operators to combine smaller expressions.*

The third paragraph in there tells us:

> *Most characters, including all letters and digits, are regular expressions that match themselves.*

and:

> *Any meta-character with special meaning may be quoted by preceding it with a backslash.*

12.3　RE meta-characters

'.' — a dot will match any *single* character *except* a `newline` control character

'[' — starts a *list* enclosed in square brackets '[...]' to match any *one* of the *list* of enclosed characters

[abc] — match *one* of the characters 'a' or 'b' or 'c' — in some user 'locale' settings this could match '[aBbCc]'

If the *first* character of the *list* is the caret or circumflex (*pointy-hat*) symbol (^) then match any character **not** in the list

Inside square brackets a pair of characters separated by a hyphen '-' or dash will match a *range* of characters

[m-q] — match one of the characters 'm' or 'n' or 'o' or 'p' or 'q'

Certain named classes of characters get predefined within bracket expressions — their names are self explanatory:

[:alnum:], [:alpha:], [:blank:], [:cntrl:], [:digit:], [:graph:], [:lower:], [:print:], [:punct:], [:space:], [:upper:] and [:xdigit:].

Note that the square bracket and the colon characters ('[:') and (':]') *surrounding* each class name is part of the symbolic name and these *must* get included in *addition* to the outer brackets of a *list* expression

Most *meta-characters* lose their special meaning inside the brackets of a *list*

To match a literal ']' place it as the *first* character in a *list*

To match a circumflex (or *pointy hat*) character place it anywhere except (other than) the *first* character in a *list*

To match a literal hyphen or dash ('-') character place it *last* in a *list*

Note: If we need to restrict the *list* to none other than those characters we enter in the *list* we can set an environment variable named 'LC_ALL' to a *value* of 'C':

```
$ export LC_ALL="C"
$ grep '[bcd]' note.txt
...
```

We could try defining our own **alias** command:

```
$ type grc
bash: type: grc: not found
$ alias grc='export LC_ALL="C" ; grep'
$ grc '[bcd]' note.txt
...
```

Does that work?

The 'export' command defines the 'LC_ALL' variable in such a way that it continues to get seen in the interactive bash shell and in new non-login command shells. Remember — one of those gets started for each Linux command we run on the command-line — and the 'grep' command will then get run in a bash shell with the environment variable 'LC_ALL' set to 'C'.

Note: Your locale could be different from mine and you may not need to use this *hack* to get the 'grep' command to operate in the way you prefer.

12.4   RE anchoring

The caret or circumflex (*pointy hat*) symbol (^) and the dollar ($) symbol are *meta-characters* that respectively match the *empty* string at the *beginning* (^) and *end* ($) of a *line*.

Side-Note: These two symbols *also* get used in the 'vim' editor to move the *cursor* to the *beginning* (^) and *end* ($) of the text on a *line* — single key smart cursor motion.

The two character symbols ('\<') and ('\>') respectively match the *empty* string at the *beginning* and *end* of a *word*.

More *meta-character* pairs get defined to match other special cases.

See 'man grep' for more details.

Assuming we still have a copy of that small shell script named 'td.sh' in our home directory:

```
$ cd
$ grep '^echo$ td.sh
echo
echo
$
```

This restricts the 'grep' command to showing us any lines that contain nothing other than the word 'echo'. No big deal for that small script.

If there was a trailing blank space after one of those 'echo' words then this 'grep' command would have displayed one line instead of two.

The same command could look through a file with hundreds and thousands of lines in moments.

12.5   RE repetition

A regular expression can get followed by a repetition operator. These operators are:

'?' — match *zero* or *one* of the preceding RE

'*' — match *zero* or *more* of the preceding RE

'+' — match *one* or *more* of the preceding RE

{n} — match preceding RE exactly 'n' times

{n,} — match preceding RE 'n' or *more* times

{,m} — match preceding RE at most 'm' times

{n,m} — match preceding RE at least 'n' times and no more than 'm' times

Other RE operations and operators cover RE concatenation, RE alternation, RE precedence and RE back-references within parenthesized subexpressions. It's a powerful information handling computing concept.

Learn to use *regular expressions* — they will serve you well.

See 'man grep' for those details.

We can use REs in other programs like the editor 'vim' and the powerful stream editor 'sed' and the 'less' paginator that gets used when we read man page information.

We can search for RE *patterns* instead of using entire strings of words and phrases.

In 'vim' and 'less' we can use the forward-slash character ('/') to start a search process then add an RE and press the Enter key to find any pattern match.

Note: Any time we invest in learning how to use the power of regular expressions will pay dividends by helping us to use other Linux tools with better efficiency.

An amazing little language called 'AWK' allows us to use REs to match what action(s) gets taken when it finds a pattern match in its input — that could come from a file or from a process pipeline.

AWK contains its own functions like 'gsub' and 'split' and 'substr' to help us make changes to the text it finds that matches what we can describe using REs.

AWK gets its name from the family name initials of its three authors — Alfred V. Aho, Brian W. Kernighan and Peter J. Weinberger.

Investigate AWK — for me it's worth its weight in gold.

See 'man awk' for lots of interesting reading.

Another exceptional tool that uses REs is the Perl scripting language — initially developed by Larry Wall. Although AWK and Perl have been around for decades their usefulness is by no means over — not in my tool box!

Another priceless feature these two languages provide is a data storage structure called 'associative arrays' — unordered collections of scalar values indexed by string subscripts or keys. Perl calls its *associative arrays* a 'hash' data structure. In Python we use a 'dictionary' data structure with '{key:value}' pairs.

Consider this small Perl script called 'count.pl' to which I made a previous reference when talking about the analysis of my work day commands. Using the '-n' option with 'cat' will number each line for easy reference:

```
$cat -n count.pl
 1 #!/usr/bin/env perl
 2 # Program: count.pl
 3 while (<>) {
 4     chop;
 5     @wrds = split;
```

```
 6    for (@wrds) {
 7        $count{$_}++
 8    }
 9 }
10 for (sort keys %count) {
11     printf "%20s %2d \n ", $_, $count{$_};
12 }
```

Line 1 has a 'hash-bang' line for perl programs and the next line is a comment.

Line 3 starts a 'while' loop statement that ends at line 9 and uses the *diamond* operator '(<>)' to read in lines of data from its standard input stream.

The 'chop;' statement on line 4 will trim off (*remove*) the trailing 'newline' character from the end of each line it reads.

Line 5 constructs and *array* or a *list* variable ('@wrds') from the *default* output of the 'split' command that uses a Perl RE — '\s' to deliver *blank space* separated words.

Lines 6 to 8 use a 'for' loop to access each value from the '@wrds' list or array — one at a time into Perl special variable '$_'.

Line 7 uses the value in '$_' as the *index* into a new *associative* array (or *hash*) called '%count' and increments ('++') the value of that array element '$count{$_}' for each *word* that's in the '@wrds' list/array.

The last three lines comprise another 'for' loop to access a sorted list of the *keys* or *indices* of the whole '%count' associative array (or *hash*) that got constructed in lines 6 to 8.

Line 11 displays the values of this 'for' loop's Perl special variable '$_' and the associated value of the indexed items from the *hash* elements ('$count{$_}').

Running this on my small shell script 'td.sh':

```
$ ./count.pl td.sh
"                   1
"Today              1
#!/usr/bin/bash     1
%F"                 1
+"%A                1
date                1
echo                2
is                  1
printf              1
```

Nothing over exciting to see here — except a count of '2' for 'echo'.

The script counts space separated *words* in its input from the file or *redirected* input specified on the command line.

The script can also take input from a *pipeline* or from a redirected ('<') input file or command substitution output — all because of the Perl '(<>)' *diamond* operator.

This small script's idea of a *word* is any string of non-blank characters — not always too helpful. The script could get extended to treat punctuation characters as word separators, too.

The documentation for Perl gets split into dozens of sections. See 'man perl' and 'man perldoc' for even more interesting reading.

To read about Perl's special '$_' variable you could run:

```
$ perldoc -v '$_'
```

Or to read about Perl's data types:

```
$ perldoc perldata
```

It's an extraordinary language with extraordinary capability.

Chapter 13

More Linux commands

The Linux system provides us with hundreds of commands to help us in almost any task we can imagine. While any one of those commands does not perform all of what we can have in mind — we have seen that there are ways we can combine these commands to produce more useful results.

13.1   Filters head & tail

If we need to handle large text files then we find software tools like the 'head' and 'tail' commands can come to our help to let us deal with selected parts of those files.

Although ultimately we will want to handle entire text data files — we can often need to extract a sample of the file to help us test a shell script or other program we want to use to prove our work process.

Imagine we have a file containing two or three hundred lines of plain text — or hundreds of thousands of lines if we need.

We can use the 'head' command to examine the first twenty lines of that with:

```
$ head -20 big-file.txt
```

To get the second set of twenty lines we can run:

```
$ head -40 big-file.txt | tail -20
```

We can run similar commands for the third and fourth and fifth and sixth groups of twenty lines, etc.

We could redirect those file segments into a series of test data files named 't1.txt', 't2.txt', 't3.txt', etc.:

```
$ head -20 big-file.txt > t1.txt
$ head -40 big-file.txt \
> | tail -20 > t2.txt
$ head -60 big-file.txt \
> | tail -20 > t3.txt
...
```

When we add the backslash symbol as the *last* character on an interactive line of **bash** shell commands and press the **Enter** key the **bash** shell will wrap onto the next line and *insert* the *greater-than* symbol ('>') to prompt and remind us it's still expecting more input from us.

Note: We must add no blank space after those line ending backslash characters to make this work — otherwise the bash shell will complain to us with an error message like "No such file or directory" before it issues our next shell prompt.

A backslash followed by a blank space would *look* like a file named with a single blank space — that we have quoted with the backslash. Bleah!

13.2   Filters cmp & diff

We can use the 'cmp' command — mnemonic for *compare* and the 'diff' command — mnemonic for *differences* to ensure we do not use the same test data over and over again.

If two files compare the *same* the 'cmp' command will give *no* output — remember *no news* is *good news* — success — there's no difference.

If the files *differ* in any way then 'cmp' will make some noise at the first point of departure it finds:

```
$ cmp t1.txt t2.txt
f1.txt f2.txt differ:  byte 1, line 1
```

We can use the 'diff' command to display the difference(s) in more detail:

```
$ diff t1.txt t2.txt | less
 . . .
 . . .
```

See 'man diff' for an explanation of the output from 'diff'.

13.3   Filters tac & rev

The 'tac' (*reverse* cat) and 'rev' (reverse the characters across a *line*) filters are unusual tools that can get used at times.

Back in chapter 7 we used two 'echo' commands to write one line and then append another line into a small file I called 'out.txt':

```
$ echo "first out" > out.txt
$ echo "next out" >> out.txt
$ cat out.txt
first out
next out
```

Using 'tac' will reverse the order of the lines. Here is the result of running the 'tac' command on 'out.txt':

```
$ tac out.txt
next out
first out
```

Using 'rev' will reverse the order of the text characters across each line. Here is the result of running the 'rev' command on 'out.txt':

```
$ rev out.txt
tuo tsrif
tuo txen
```

Those commands did not change the content of the file 'out.txt':

```
$ cat out.txt
first out
next out
```

We can use 'out.txt' or any other plain text file to illustrate how good the 'tac' and 'rev' filters do their job:

```
$ tac out.txt | rev | tac | rev > out.trtr
$ ls -go out.txt out.trtr
-rw-r----- 1 19 Jun 27 16:14 out.trtr
-rw-r----- 1 19 Jun 27 16:01 out.txt
```

Running and repeating those two commands again — in any order should reproduce the original text.

The output files have the same size — that is a good start.

Do they contain the same content"

```
$ cmp out.txt out.trtr
```

No output — that's good.

There's no difference to report. The files compare as the same.

Remember: No news is good news.

Why ever would you want to use the commands 'tac' and 'rev' in real life?

Consider this — having finished a lengthy report document or computer program our reviewers provide us with lists of their suggested updates and amendments.

Their suggestions could include page numbers, section numbers, paragraph numbers and line numbers referring to the locations where amendments need to get considered and made.

If we started work on the suggestions of one reviewer and made amendments before looking at the suggestions of the next and any other reviewers — the line numbers and other reference points could get difficult to locate.

If we were to start at the top of their combined list and work our way down to the end then if we added or subtracted any significant parts of text those reference numbers further down the file could become more difficult to identify in an updated document.

One way around this issue is to start with the last item first and work our way back up the list instead — towards amendment references at the top of our lengthy document or program.

Here's one place for the use for 'tac' — to produce their suggestions list in reverse order. It's easy to write a shell command (or script) to read a *reversed* list and fire up our editor (like 'vim') at each of those referenced lines in turn!

Say we had a small file called 'ed-lns.txt' containing a list of the necessary line edits for a file called 'new.doco':

```
$ cat ed-lns.txt
32
83
147
239
```

We could run this in our interactive bash shell:

```
$ for lno in $(tac ed-lns.txt) ; do
> vim +$lno new.doco
> done
```

All we need do is make the necessary edit(s) at the line where our *cursor* lands — and then *exit* from the editor.

In 'vim' I'd use the *last-line* command ':wq' — mnemonic for *write* and *quit* — or the *short-hand* '{Shift}+{Z}+{Z}'.

The 'for-do-done' loop moves to the next *value* of '$lno' parameter it gets from the command substitution part '$(tac ed-lns.txt)' and re-runs the editor.

Easy — we could write a script to automate that.

This is one of the reasons I prefer to run my editor on the command-line inside my Terminal windows and tabs — rather than firing up a GUI 'Editor' window from an *icon* with its File menus, etc.

That works for me.

Using the 'rev' filter can come into play where we need to consider reverse sort orders in unusual circumstances.

13.4   Auto-reporting

The steam editor 'sed' helps us to make changes to text on the fly.

Why would we want to do that?

Earlier we used the 'tr' (*translate*) command to convert the colon (':') characters between the directory paths in our 'PATH' variable into *newline* characters to get each path displayed on a separate line.

That was useful for doing what we needed to make that list easier to read.

Using 'sed' we can use REs (*regular expressions*) to locate characters or words or phrases in its input stream (from a file or a pipeline) and convert or change or delete or extend the text to make it more readable/understandable — in almost any way we may want.

Suppose we had a small template file to help us report the results of the testing procedures we conduct on the shell scripts and other programs we develop and then deploy for more widespread use.

Management requires that we provide assurance reports to show the results of our product testing and need us to flag any potential issues and errors *before* we release updated products for general use and deliver these to other users and unsuspecting customers.

The products could need to get sent back to the developer(s) for more analysis and repair work!

The test analysts use an automated test harness that
conducts test cases and reports a pass or fail for each coded
test case.

How can we take those product test results and use these to
auto-complete a report for management — on demand?

Suppose the testing process emits terse messages like this:

```
01:cmd no opts/args:pass
02:cmd line bad opts:pass
03:cmd line good opts:pass
04:cmd line bad args:pass
05:cmd line good args:pass
06:cmd idat bad:pass
07:cmd odat bad vals:pass
08:cmd odat bad errs:fail
09:cmd idat good:pass
10:cmd odat good vals:pass
11:cmd odat good errs:pass
```

We want to read each line of data emitted by the testing
process and use the colon separated field values to help
produce a more readable document for management.

13.5   Stream editor sed

The *stream* editor 'sed' command includes a *search and
replace* instruction that can get composed and used like this:

```
$ sed -e 's/RE/text/g' file.txt
```

The 'sed' command can handle more than one of these *edit*
instructions and I find a convenient way to do that is to
add a backslash character before the file name and press the
Enter key to wrap onto the next line(s) with more edit parts:

```
$ sed -e 's/RE/text/g' \
      -e 's/RE/text/g' \
      -e 's/RE/text/g' file.txt
```

The 'sed' command makes one pass over its input — one line at a time and executes each of those '-e' edit commands in turn to find and make changes to the text.

To parse the test results data and make those terse information strings more readable we could use:

```
$ sed -e 's/opts/options/g' \
      -e 's/args/arguments/g' \
      -e 's/idat/input data/g' \
      -e 's/odat/output data/g' \
      -e 's/fmt/format/g' \
      -e 's/vals/values/g' \
      -e 's/errs/error messages/g' \
      -e 's/:pass/ --> pass/g' \
      -e 's/:fail/ --> FAIL/g' \
      -e 's/:/ /g' file.txt
```

We can put those lines (after a 'hash-bang' line) into a shell script named 'report.sh' — without the first '$' prompt character and then use the 'chmod' command to make it executable and run it on the test result data file to produce:

```
$ ./report.sh
01 cmd no options/arguments --> pass
02 cmd line bad options --> pass
03 cmd line good options --> pass
04 cmd line bad arguments --> pass
05 cmd line good arguments --> pass
06 cmd inp-data bad --> pass
07 cmd out-data bad values --> pass
08 cmd out-data bad error text --> FAIL
```

```
09 cmd inp-data good --> pass
10 cmd out-data good values --> pass
11 cmd out-data good error text --> pass
```

Nothing extra special. I hope you get the gist of the idea. The final report could need to get tabulated with headers and footers and with dates and other details embedded — no problem.

We could use two or three lines of bash shell code to call one or more AWK script(s) to perform all kinds of actions to help us achieve precisely what we need.

13.6   The file command

There can be times when we need to know what data type content a file has inside.

Do we have files that contain any data type *indicator* suffix strings like — '.awk' *or* '.aux' *or* '.bib' *or* '.c' *or* '.cfg' *or* '.cpp' *or* '.csh' *or* '.csv' *or* '.dat' *or* '.deb' *or* '.doc' *or* '.docx' *or* '.dvi' *or* '.eml' *or* '.eps' *or* '.epub' *or* '.ftn' *or* '.gv' *or* '.gz' *or* '.html' *or* '.iso' *or* '.jpg' *or* '.js' *or* '.json' *or* '.ksh' *or* '.lex' *or* '.log' *or* '.lua' *or* '.ly' *or* '.md' *or* '.midi' *or* '.mp3' *or* '.ogg' *or* '.odp' *or* '.ods' *or* '.pdf' *or* '.pl' *or* '.png' *or* '.ppt' *or* '.ps' *or* '.py' *or* '.R' *or* '.rb' *or* '.sh' *or* '.sql' *or* '.sty' *or* '.tar' *or* '.tcl' *or* '.tex' *or* '.toc' *or* '.txt' *or* '.wav' *or* '.xlsx' *or* '.xml' *or* '.xz' *or* '.zip' — *or* any others we could use?

There's no guarantee that a file contains what the file suffix says or what we imagine or what we could hope it does.

There's a utility command called 'file' that can help us to determine the data type a file contains:

```
$ file .bashrc
.bashrc:  ASCII text
$ file count.pl
count.pl:  Perl script text executable
$ file tee.txt
tee.txt:  Unicode text, UTF-8 text
$ file wav/faith.wav
wav/faith.wav:  RIFF (little-endian) data,
WAVE audio, Microsoft PCM, 16 bit, stereo
44100 Hz
```

We could use a 'grep' command to search for keywords like 'ASCII' or 'Perl' or 'text' or 'WAVE', etc.

The 'grep' command returns a '0' (*success*) exit status when it finds a match.

Remember we can check the exit status of the *last* command using the special '?' variable — its *value* is '$?'.

It contains the exit status value of the previous command that ran in the current shell — interactively or inside a shell script.

13.7   The sort filter

While we have seen the Linux 'sort' command before — it contains over thirty (30) different command-line *options* to get it to perform in wonderful ways to help us *sort* our lines of data.

For example, suppose we wanted to get a list of file names sorted in alphabetical order by their file type suffix strings — instead of the whole file names.

An 'ls' listing shows we have these files:

```
$ ls
```

```
f1.abc    f4.zip    file1.txt
f2.ly     f5.jpg    file2.txt
f3.c
```

We want to see 'f1.abc' *first* and 'f4.zip' *last*:

```
$ ls -1 | sort -t .   -k 2
f1.abc
f3.c
f5.jpg
f2.ly
file1.txt
file2.txt
f4.zip
```

The '-1' (*hyphen or dash one*) option given to the 'ls'
command requests the list of file names to get displayed as
one on each line.

The two options given to the sort command are '-t {SEP}'
to use 'SEP' — a dot ('.') as the field *transition* separator
(instead of the usual blank space for plain text) and then '-k
{KEY}' where we can specify *key number* 2.

Given that my file names almost *always* contain one single
dot ('.') character — right before the file type suffix I expect
the *second* dot separated field on each line that gets output
from the 'ls -1' command is the file type character (like 'c')
or string (like 'txt').

It's possible to specify more complicated sort keys!

See 'man sort' and *search* for "/KEYDEF".

If there were files names containing more than one dot —
we could choose to use a bit of AWK code to move the *last*
(file type) field to become the first field on each line and
then call 'sort' without the options followed a bit more

```
```

AWK code to restore the positions of the file type suffix strings.

13.8   Shared file access

When we work on Linux computers with more than one user we can find there are times when we need shared access to files.

One way to do that is to change the third set of 'rwx' file permission bits to give the necessary access for *all* others.

Often that is *not* the best idea.

We could work in a research group where we need to share intermediate results with others *in* our group. It could be *inappropriate* to let *all* other users have open access to *unfinished* reports and/or *preliminary* analysis details, etc.

What can we do?

Files have both the owner (**user**) and **group** name identifiers we can see by running an 'ls -l' command.

We can use another command called 'chgrp' — mnemonic for *change group* to change the group name identifier of a file or directory that we own.

The group we choose needs to pre-exist.

Say we want to use a group identity of '**res**' — mnemonic for *research*.

We can check if that group exists by using a '**grep**' command to search through the '/etc/group' file — where the group identifiers and their lists of one or more members gets stored:

```
$ grep '^res:' /etc/group
```

We search for lines that start (^) with the group name 'res' followed by a colon (:) character.

No output means the group 'res' doesn't yet exist — we need to make that.

There's an *administrator* command called 'addgroup' to make a new group identifier. To make a new group called 'res' — we need to run — or ask the system *administrator* to run (if that is not us):

```
$ sudo addgroup res
```

There's another *administrator* command called 'adduser' to help us add an existing user to the new group. To add the user 'clu' to that new group we can run:

```
$ sudo adduser clu res
```

We can run that to add other users to the 'res' group.

On large multi-user systems we could need to go through a formal request process — getting that approved by management, etc.

These users will need log out and sign in again to see their new group membership get reported by the 'id' or 'groups' commands.

Any file we *own* that needs to get access that's restricted to ourself and *members* of the 'res' group needs to have it's group identifier changed to 'res' by running that 'chgrp' command:

```
$ chgrp res prelim-results.txt
```

The final commands we need to run will involve changing the permission bits for the group (g) to *add* (+) the *read* (r) access bit and to *remove* (-) all permissions from all others:

```
$ chmod g+r prelim-results.txt
$ chmod o-o prelim-results.txt
```

To make the files available to the 'res' group we could need
to change the group ownership of our '$HOME' directory and
any sub-directories to which a group member will need access
to search for the group access files.

An alternative method is to make a special 'res' directory
in another part of the Linux file system — or generate a *new*
user named 'res' and use their '$HOME' directory area for the
'res' *group* files.

Suppose we make a 'res' directory in our $HOME directory
where we want to store the files to which the 'res' group has
access:

```
$ cd
$ mkdir res
```

We get to own the directory and by default will have the
read, write and *execute* permissions there — enabling us to
copy, edit, move and *remove* files.

Next we run the 'chgrp' command to change the group
identity of '~' (our '$HOME' directory) and the new 'res'
directory:

```
$ chgrp res ~ res
```

Then we use 'chmod' to permit both *read* and *exectute*
permissions for the 'res' group:

```
$ chmod g+rx ~ res
```

```
```

Note: For a directory the *execute* permission means we have access to *search* (or list the contents of) the directory to show other file system objects — if any.

Next we move the '`prelim-results.txt`' file into the '`res`' directory:

```
$ mv prelim-results.txt res
```

Other members of the '`res`' group should now get the access they need to *read* the file.

Without granting *write* access to the '`res`' group means those group members do not have permission to make any changes there.

Essentially — they can look at the file(s) — they don't get permission to touch (or make *changes* to) the file(s) — without our permission.

Warning: A member in the shared group who can *read* a file can also take a *copy* of that file — they become the *owner* of that file *copy* and can choose to do what they will with that!

This access method relies upon a great degree of trust. If we can't trust those with whom we live and/or work — then we get caught between a rock and a hard place.

Why don't people see the reasons for the necessary levels of trust and responsibility and integrity?

Do they understand their responsibility to keep the group communications at the necessary level of privileged shared access?

It takes one untrustworthy person to break our trust. It takes great effort to restore our trust — if ever.

It takes great effort to build a more secure system — at times we need to make *set-group* processes to control access to shared resources and make those *group* processes limit what access the users can get.

See 'man sg' and 'man newgrp' for more details.

We can use these techniques to grant shared file access to other family members on our personal Linux PC where appropriate — to give them *read* access.

For example they might like to have access to our stash of family photo image files — or the family memoirs you've been writing or anything else you choose.

Chapter 14

My working method

Here is an image showing part of the directory and sub-directory structure that I use for my software development work:

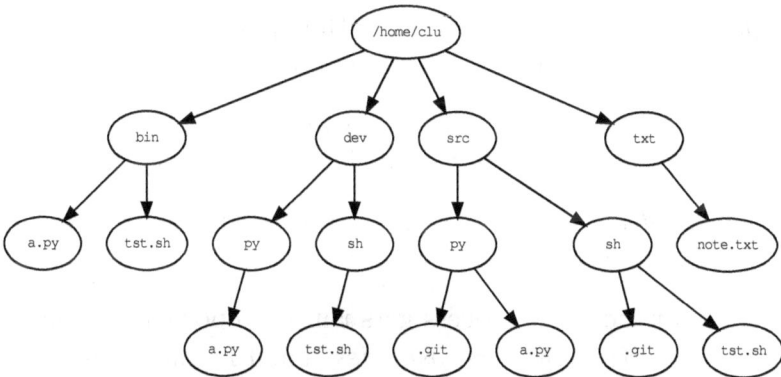

I tend to keep a *development* version of my scripts in my "dev" sub-directories and a *tested source* version in my "src" sub-directories and then the final executable version gets copied back to my own '$HOME/bin' directory for my day to day use.

When I find the need to modify or enhance a script or fix an uncovered bug — I will work on the *development* version until I am happy with the result.

I use the clever Linux program called 'diff' — mnemonic for *differences* — to display the changes I have made between the *development* version and the *bin* or *source* version of the script.

There are GUI versions of 'diff' like the KDE 'kdiff3' command and the older 'mgdiff' and my favourite called 'tkdiff' — this needs the Tcl/Tk libraries ('tcl8.5' and 'tk8.5') installed.

See: https://tkdiff.sourceforge.io/

This step lets me see that I have updated the version number and have added a suitable comment or comments to describe what I have done.

When I have performed the *testing* I need to do — to assure myself the update works as expected then I copy the *development* version across to the appropriate *source* ('src/py' or 'src/sh', etc.) sub-directory.

The next part of the process uses commands from the trustworthy 'git' distributed version control system.

My *modified* file gets a 'git add' process run on it to make it a *staged* item ready to get *committed* to the 'git' database.

Next a 'git commit' process gets run to deposit my *staged* updates into the '.git' *repositories* that I maintain in each of those ('src/...') locations.

The initial concepts behind and the design for 'git' got initiated by Linus Torvalds while he was developing and coordinating enhancements to the Linux kernel system — complex software that needs constant updates and hence the ability to keep track of hundreds and thousands of changes.

A 'git' repository can maintain *parallel* branches of development if required and can *merge* together those branches when appropriate development and testing and any *conflict resolution* gets done and then gets our approval — it's a most capable version control system.

See 'man git' for more details — there is extensive documentation to read there. See 'man gittutorial' to get started.

Now I expect that sounds like a lot of work. The good thing is that most of these steps get encapsulated in my own development and release *scripts* and *aliases*.

I run a *script* or an *alias* at the appropriate time to instigate the action or actions I want to see taken on a specified file.

Following this sort of procedure helps me keep control of what I am doing and what I have completed — helps me see what is useful and what needs more work.

At last count I have over 500 scripts in my '$HOME/bin' directory that got written and developed by me — since I started using Linux in 1994.

That equates to about one (1) new script each month — there's plenty of other work going on with time to spare.

I could not have done that without developing and refining my software handling procedures over the years. I started slow and built small improvements as time went by.

What ever do I do with all those scripts?

If I am truthful I expect most of these have outlived their usefulness. My requirements can change from one week to the next and writing a new small piece of **bash** shell code can provide a solution in next to no time.

There's a small number of scripts that got started with their development in the first year or two — and I still use these almost every day — even now.

To me that's most encouraging. I know the small amounts of

effort I put into my shell script writing can pay dividends for years to come.

These shell scripts continue to work in the way I programmed them to — even though my Linux system has undergone over 22 major updates.

Most of those updates happen in an incremental manner and the impact on me — the Linux user — is minimal. At worst a minute or two every other day or week — except when I choose to upgrade to the latest LTS release if that needs to happen on its own.

I keep small fragments or snippets of shell script code to help me write other scripts. For instance there's a main one called 'start.sh' that helps me get going on almost any new shell script with a framework that I prefer to use.

If a shell script needs to perform a significant amount of work and needs to provide the user with more than one option then I will use that 'start.sh' script because it contains code to handle command-line options using the 'getopt' process I prefer (rather than 'getopts') and it handles lists of command-line arguments with a bash shell 'while-do-done' loop method I have trusted for years.

If I find myself looking at a shell script I wrote years ago there will be other fragments of code I can read into the old script to help me update that to use my latest coding standards and use better code blocks that I continuously try to improve as time goes by.

In Linux there's a clever utility called 'shellcheck' — a static analysis and linting tool for sh/bash scripts.

We can run 'shellcheck' on our script(s) and follow the advice it gives:

```
$ shellcheck td.sh
```

Remember, no news is good news!

I use 'shellcheck' to help me keep the content in my shell scripts conforming to most of the suggestions it provides — except when I have a good reason to use any personal variation to those guidelines.

For example, in an interactive script when I need to *prompt* the user to press the 'Enter' key to *continue* after I have displayed information I want them to read — I could write:

```
printf "Press the Enter key to continue:   "
# shellcheck disable=SC2034
read -er Resp
```

Without the '# shellcheck disable=SC2034' comment line the 'shellcheck' program will forever complain about my use of the *unreferenced* variable I have called 'Resp' given to the 'read' command.

All my script needs — is to get an 'Enter' key *response* from the user.

Reading 'man bash' the 'read' command can get called *without* a variable like 'Resp' — in that case the *response* from the user gets assigned to a variable named 'REPLY'.

I use the variable 'Resp' because is certain cases I will want to make use of what the user responds — when I ask the user to specify one from a certain choice when I could prompt them with:

```
printf "Continue (Y)es or (N)o?   "
read -er Resp
case "$Resp" in
    [Yy]*) ;;
    [Nn]*) exit 0 ;;
    *) exit 9 ;;
esac
```

The fact that I will not always want to use that variable for anything other than helping my script to wait for a response from the user is my choice!

It's good to know I can help the 'shellcheck' program to ignore that — when I choose.

I am exceeding glad that the original Bourne Shell ('sh') and now the Bourne-again Shell ('bash') is so expressive and capable of performing the necessary conditional logic tests with looping constructs and variable and file handling features to make a programmer's life more productive.

A shell script is not the answer to everything — at times we need to use a more powerful solution. Shell scripts sit with perfection between the layers of computing capability provided by the powerful Linux kernel and those two important design concepts of the *file system* and the *process*.

In Linux a file is a file — it does not much matter what the content.

We use the same utility programs like 'ls' and 'cp' and 'mv' to handle music files and PDF files and plain text files without the need to be too concerned about the file content — until we want to listen to the music or print or display the PDF files or pull apart and re-assemble the plain text files that can be letters or memos or shell scripts or Lilypond music notation files or C++ or C programs or Python scripts or HTML web page files or Java programs or SQL query scripts or data inputs to database files or . . .

The capable Linux system provides us with thousands — yes thousands of resources we can download and use to handle almost every data file type and content we can imagine.

There's a 'Software Manager' tool to help us install new applications on our Linux PCs — although I find this GUI program more difficult to use than other methods.

My head does not deal well with an avalanche of icons!

For years I have been using the 'synaptic' (another GUI) package manager to help me locate and install extra pieces of software for my Linux PCs.

Whether it's an application to play music or to manage an SQL database or to help me with my programming or writing or to convert data from one format to another — 'synaptic' makes it easy for me to find what I need.

For example the 'ImageMagick' suite of command-line tools like 'convert' to help *convert* bitmap image file formats and *resize, blur, crop, despeckle* an *dither* an image — and more.

Or the GUI 'audacity' program to help me edit the wave files ('*.wav') for my recorded music.

Or a command-line program called 'cmus' to help me play a selection of other music from my collection of favourite songs and instrumental pieces — there's a 'cmus-tutorial' to help us get started in a minute or two.

There are command-line programs like 'apt' and 'apt-get' and 'dpkg' to help us install new software and to update the now installed software packages on our systems. Each of these has its own **man** page.

The synaptic GUI is a front-end for the 'apt' package management system.

When I last checked, the categories of software packages from which we can choose to install programs and utilities with the 'synaptic' package manager included these 55 items:

> 'Amateur Radio' and 'Communications' and
> 'Cross Platform' and 'Databases' and 'Debug'
> and 'Development' and 'Documentation' and
> 'Editors' and 'Education' and 'Electronics'
> and 'Email' and 'Embedded Devices' and
> 'Fonts' and 'Games Amusement' and 'GNOME'

and 'GNU R' and 'Gnustep Desktop' and 'Go
Programming' and 'Graphics' and 'Haskell
Programming' and 'Internationalization' and
'Interpreted Computer Languages' and 'JAVA
Programming' and 'JavaScript Programming'
and 'KDE Desktop' and 'Kernel and modules'
and 'Libraries' and 'Lisp Programming'
and 'Localization' and 'Mathematics' and
'Meta Packages' and 'Miscellaneous' and
'Mono/CLI Infrastructure' and 'Multimedia'
and 'Networking' and 'Newsgroup' and 'OCaml
Programming' and 'Perl Programming' and 'PHP
Programming' and 'Python Programming' and
'Ruby Programming' and 'Rust Programming'
and 'Science' and 'Shells' and 'System Admin'
and 'TeX Authoring' and 'Text Processing' and
'Utilities' and 'Version Control Systems' and
'Video software' and 'Web Servers' and 'Word
Processing' and 'World Wide Web' and 'Xfce
Desktop' and the 'Zope/Plone Environment'.

There should be something of interest to most of us.

14.1   Clear horizons

In Linux it's rare to get stuck with no way forward or no way
out. We could need to read another part of a **man** page or
debug a small piece of **bash** shell script code to help us make
progress — it does not take long.

We get better at this with practise. It provides stimulating
reward for our intellect when we make progress — it's fun.

One of the most important items for me to remember is
to produce adequate documentation describing why I have
taken one path over another or what was the catalyst for my

choice of using the method I did over other ways I might have pursued instead.

It's inevitable we will find a need to return to the snippets of code we write to solve a similar problem or build a bigger and better product with more features and enhancements — we need to have access to accurate and up to date documentation describing the parts we found awkward to solve or complete.

I try to put lots of comments in my code.

These do not slow down the execution of our code. As soon as the bash shell interpreter sees a hash ('#') symbol it automatically skips the rest of the line — that's a rapid operation.

Start the comments in column one (1) or as the first item after blank space indentation(s) to help both our readability and the **bash** shell to decide '*found a* **hash**' — *skip to the next line!*

Do not expect other people to figure out *why we did* what we did without a hint or two about the reasons that motivated or cemented our choice of one process or procedure over another.

If ever we need to come back and revisit our own code — we will thank ourself it we left behind helpful comments to describe more of the fine details — what do those variable names mean?

Supplementing our own growing list of resources — aliases or shell scripts or applications — we have access to thousands of packages and pieces of software we can install on our Linux PCs.

If we do not like what we install — we can always run an *un-install* process.

If ever the list of available Linux packages is insufficient

— we have access to more resources from open software developers all around the world.

A brief Internet search with selected keywords can produce more options to investigate within moments.

We still need to follow Internet security guidelines and refrain from following links to insecure web pages — that's common sense.

For a part of my working life at a world class climate research group we needed to download and analyse an enormous volume (`terabytes`) of 'netCDF' data files and use tools like the 'cdo' — Climate Data Operators from the Max Planck Institute for Meteorology to help our scientists make sense of their comparisons of data from dozens of different weather models from other Meteorological sites around the world.

Linux was more than up to the task as the operating of choice for the complex computational analyses we ran on supercomputers harnessing hundreds of compute nodes — each with dozens of CPU cores.

For me Linux represents the best computer system I have ever used.

To have Linux running on my own personal computer has provided me with an extraordinary functional capability above and beyond my computation needs — because it provides me with an almost endless toolbox of commands and utilities and applications I can use to solve my requirements for information handling.

Using Linux is never a chore — it's a sheer delight.

Chapter 15

Using snippets

I have mentioned my use of *snippets* of shell script code
and code for other interpreted languages I use like Perl and
Python and R and Tcl/Tk.

When I need to start writing a new script — I will often use
one of my *starter* files named 'start.{pl,py,R,sh,tcl}'.

If I were to start from scratch every time this would add a
couple of hours or more to the development time.

It's easy to delete ten or twenty lines of code from my starter
script if I decide those are unnecessary. It could take longer if
I needed to re-write them when I did want the functionality
of those lines.

I'm a firm believer in using '*snippets*' anywhere I can — it's
not *exclusive* to programming.

For example, if we need to construct a form letter or a
business memo or a routine report or any number of other
documents where one version will appear *similar* to the next
version — with dates and times updated — with different
name and address details — with different parameters
and values — these can be prime candidates for the use of
snippets to help construct what we need.

A memo needs a header with the *sender* and *recipient* details — plus current date and/or time information. It will need the text for the body of the memo — and other component parts as required.

Each of these can get thought of as a *snippet* and could get handled by a *builder* script written in our preferred scripting language.

Small projects like these need thoughtful design and construction and testing considerations.

An hour or two of work can help us produce a shell script to assemble a form letter or a memo that could need to get sent to tens or hundreds or thousands of recipients.

After testing and any bug fixing — by the end of the day you could have something of use.

The resulting shell script will often need more tweaks with time and usage and as the task requirements change or extend in the future.

When the body of the document changes next month or next week or tomorrow we can substitute the updated body text and re-run the builder script to get the next document run — out the door.

Other parts of such a system will generally need database maintenance to remove old contacts and add new contact details, etc.

The database can be as simple as a plain text file or as complicated as an SQL or other dedicated database system.

There is a need for an approvals process from management — for the project and associated scheduling of print runs and couriers and delivery services and other necessary control and management functions.

No matter what my work involves — snippets of code and

text often make my life easier.

In my spare time I think I'll try using snippets to help me construct more Lilypond music notation files to help me with my music.

Another project for a rainy day!

Making use of *process* i/o redirection and the ability to construct process pipelines to extend and customise the chains of processing my shell scripts can perform — gives me a capability I find difficult or near impossible to achieve in any of the other computer systems I have tried to use.

Learning to harness the power of the RE (*regular expression*) will pay dividends well into the future — I am always delighted when these provide the answer to yet another problem.

Making use of a handful of the methods I have discussed can make all the difference to a project or business that struggles to meet its deadlines and targets.

Freeing up human resources to focus on difficult issues that need human interaction makes sense to me.

Automating repeatable processes makes sense to me.

Utilising available computer resources makes sense to me.

Yes — that takes people power too.

The extensive Linux tool-box of standard *commands* and tools to help write customised *scripts* and easy to type *aliases* makes sense to me.

Starting slow and building capability as we learn and absorb information about the flexibility and capability of Linux make sense to me.

Before we realise we will have amassed a body of knowledge to help us handle our information processing tasks with more ease.

When we hit a snag we have 'man' pages and 'info' pages and *tutorial* programs and on-line documents we can turn to for almost every need.

Anything we perceive to be *unfriendly* in Linux soon becomes closer than a friend as we come to rely upon the power and the repeatability these *trustworthy — work together —* software tools provide.

If we could learn everything there is to know about Linux in next to no time we would find we would tire of its inability to support our needs.

Instead I have been working with and learning about Linux for decades and I never grow tired of discovering new features and learning more ways it can help me on a continual basis.

I wish you well in your Linux pursuits.

Each to their own. We need to find what works for us.

By the same author

Nonfiction

Epub

The Miracle Working God
Depictions of the miracles in my life
2025, ISBN 9791764057868
.

Love, Joy, Peace
Living a better life by the Grace of God
2025, ISBN 9791764057844
.

Glory to God Everywhere You Are There
Describes the origins of my simple song of praise
2025, ISBN 9781764057820
.

Jesus Says You Must Be Born Again
The most important information the world affords
2025, ISBN 9781764057813

Nonfiction

Paperback

The Miracle Working God
Depictions of the miracles in my life
2025, ISBN 9791764057875

.

Love, Joy, Peace
Living a better life by the Grace of God
2025, ISBN 9791764057851

.

Glory to God Everywhere You Are There
Describes the origins of my simple song of praise
2025, ISBN 9781764057837

.

Jesus Says You Must Be Born Again
The most important information the world affords
2025, ISBN 9781764057806

.

Paul's Question
Have you received the Holy Spirit?
2023, ISBN 9798857128381

.

Linux Bread Crumbs
Learn to use Linux
2023, ISBN 9798364005830

.

To Day If You Will Hear His Voice
Believe in God
2022, ISBN 9798831130669

.

Take Another Look
Please take another look
2022, ISBN 9798437605554

.

Song Lyrics
Notes and lyrics for 16 of my songs
2022, ISBN 9798434494120

Fiction

Paperback

The Ravenscroft Algorithm
Fictitious cyber crime
2022, ISBN 9798842106202

.

Broke Reef
Fictitious shipwreck on a W.Aust. Reef
2022, ISBN 9798428316940